...ited States, in order to form a more perfect Union, establish justice, ...ote the general Welfare, and secure the Blessings of Liberty to ourselves ...United States of America.

...a Congress of the United States, which shall consist of a Senate and House

...bers chosen every second Year by the People of the several States, and the Electors ...ous Branch of the State Legislature.

...to the Age of twenty five Years, and been seven Years a Citizen of the United States, ...hall be chosen.

...al States which may be included within this Union, according to their respective ...Persons, including those bound to Service for a Term of Years, and excluding Indians ...e made within three Years after the first Meeting of the Congress of the United States, ...all by Law direct. The Number of Representatives shall not exceed one for every ...d until such enumeration shall be made, the State of New Hampshire shall be ...e Plantations one, Connecticut five, New York six, New Jersey four, Pennsylvania ...uth Carolina five, and Georgia three.

...Executive Authority thereof shall issue Writs of Election to fill such Vacancies. ...icers; and shall have the sole Power of Impeachment.
...lors from each State, chosen by the Legislature thereof, for six Years; and each

...st Election, they shall be divided as equally as may be into three Classes. The Seats ...nd Year, of the second Class at the Expiration of the fourth Year, and of the third ...second Year; and if Vacancies happen by Resignation, or otherwise, during the ...r Appointments until the next Meeting of the Legislature, which shall then fill

...of thirty Years, and been nine Years a Citizen of the United States, and who shall

...but shall have no Vote, unless they be equally divided.
...pore, in the Absence of the Vice President, or when he shall exercise the Office of

...n sitting for that Purpose, they shall be on Oath or Affirmation. When the Presid... ...nvicted without the Concurrence of two thirds of the Members present.
...removal from Office, and disqualification to hold and enjoy any Office of honor, ...less be liable and subject to Indictment, Trial, Judgment and Punishment,

We, the People

THE STORY OF
THE UNITED STATES CAPITOL
ITS PAST AND ITS PROMISE

THE UNITED STATES CAPITOL
HISTORICAL SOCIETY

In Cooperation With
THE NATIONAL GEOGRAPHIC SOCIETY

Washington, D. C.
1967

Produced by the National Geographic Society as a public service.

Lonnelle Aikman, *Author*

Jules B. Billard
Editorial Director

Robert L. Breeden
Design and Production Director

George F. Mobley and Joseph J. Scherschel, *Photography*

James R. Whitney, *Director, printing and engraving;* Donald J. Crump, *Assistant, design and production;* Geraldine Linder, Margaret S. Dean, *Photographic research;* Margery G. Dunn, Mary Ann Harrell, Patricia G. Rosenborg, *Editorial research;* Johanna G. Farren, Tamsin Griffeth, *Geographic research;* Sabine D. Parks, *Index*—all, National Geographic staff.

Mario E. Campioli, Thomas F. Clancy, Florian H. Thayn (Office of the Architect of the Capitol), Norma Greene and Lillian R. Kessel, *Manuscript and production assistance.*

Robert G. Dunphy, Sergeant at Arms, Senate; Lewis Deschler, Parliamentarian, House of Representatives; Carl S. Fogle, Office of the Architect of the Capitol; *Photographic arrangements.*

OFFICE OF THE ARCHITECT OF THE CAPITOL

STATUE OF FREEDOM *towers in enduring bronze above the Capitol Dome. Sculptor Thomas Crawford planned her as "Armed Liberty" with the soft cap of freed Roman slaves, but changed her to "Freedom" with helmet of eagle head and feathers after objections by Jefferson Davis. The 19½-foot, 7½-ton figure was erected in 1863. Its plaster original, from which the statue's five sections were cast, stands in the Smithsonian Institution.*

Foreword

THE UNITED STATES Capitol Historical Society presents this book as a service to history and the American heritage. In its pages is compressed the story of the majestic edifice that is our Capitol—how it came about, how it grew, and why it stands as a symbol in stone of the success of our Republic.

William Wirt Henry, descendant of Patrick Henry, reminded us, in 1893 at the 100th anniversary of the laying of the cornerstone of the Capitol, that "For more than a century we have demonstrated, as no other people have ever done before, our capacity for self-government. Our Federal system has been tested in peace and in war, and by violent forces from without and within, yet every fiber has stood the strain, and its perfect adaptation to our needs under all circumstances has been demonstrated."

Since then the evidence of the tough sinews that make a people great has accumulated many-fold. We have found to be true what a former Member of Congress, Rufus Choate, once said: "We have built no national temples but the Capitol. We consult no common oracle but the Constitution."

It is on the level of the dignity of these utterances that this book was conceived as a public service by the United States Capitol Historical Society. It is brought to publication in accordance with the Society's aims as an educational organization—its membership open to everyone everywhere —to foster through the story of the Capitol an understanding of the richness and inspiration of American history.

This book is a labor of love and of pride. Infinite pains have been taken to make it an accurate and graphic portrait of a structure within whose walls—through contention and through compromise, sometimes brilliantly and sometimes not so brilliantly, by pronouncement and by painful progress—a Government truly "of the people" has evolved.

Producing this book would hardly have been possible without the vision, enthusiastic encouragement, and unselfish interest of Melville Bell Grosvenor, President and Editor, and Melvin M. Payne, Executive Vice President and Secretary, of the National Geographic Society—or without the efforts of the dedicated and able talent in the organization they direct. A debt of gratitude, too, is owed to a legion of others who have added their advice and their abilities in bringing the book about.

Those who labored in this work hope the effort will stand out as a contribution to the advancement of American ideals, and that it will serve to strengthen faith in the American experience. This book, like the Capitol itself, is for people everywhere who cherish freedom. Here is evidence of the struggles that have been made—and the struggles and sacrifices that must yet be made—to keep the goal of equality of opportunity, of justice, and of freedom alive for all in the world.

Fred Schwengel

President, U. S. Capitol Historical Society

GREAT SEAL *of the United States—an impression from the original die on a commission given George Washington, 1782.*

CONTENTS

INTRODUCTION

A Place

"IT IS NATURAL enough to suppose that the center and heart of America is the Capitol," wrote Hawthorne on a Washington visit in 1862, "and certainly, in its outward aspect, the world has not many statelier or more beautiful edifices...."

The novelist saw the building almost complete, for the next year Crawford's Freedom was lifted atop the Dome. He could not then assert what all would say now, that the Capitol is the best-loved and most-revered building in America. But he was right in stating that its combination of dignity, harmony, and utility made it a fit embodiment of the highest traits of the Republic. Thornton's classic design, stamped with the approval of Washington and Jefferson, so happily expressed the majesty of our democracy that most of the state capitols reared since have echoed its lines. This, we may say, is the spirit of America in stone.

Doubtless everyone, gazing at the Dome completed amid rigors of civil war, or entering the Rotunda where Lincoln, Garfield, McKinley, Kennedy, and the Unknowns lay in state, thinks first of the august penumbra of history which enwraps the structure.

On its steps nearly all the Presidents since Jackson have been inaugurated. This is where Lafayette was welcomed as symbol of one epochal alliance, and Winston Churchill as partner in another. In the old House wing, now Statuary Hall, every visitor must feel moved at the spot where John Quincy Adams sank under his mortal stroke in 1848. Who can enter the President's Room without reflecting, "Here it was that

# of Resounding Deeds

Lincoln indomitably defied his Senate leaders by refusing to sign the radical Wade-Davis bill upon Reconstruction."

Some rooms are heavy with history. In the Old Senate Chamber, occupied from Buchanan's day by the Supreme Court, Webster replied to Hayne. The treaty closing the Mexican War was ratified. Clay and Calhoun battled over the compromise of 1850. And great Court decisions from the legal tender cases under Grant to the NIRA case under Roosevelt in 1935 were handed down.

Many of the transactions witnessed by Capitol walls still lift the hearts of men. Here Adams battled for the right of petition, and when one opponent offered a resolution for his censure as a traitor, he demanded that the clerk read the first paragraph of the Declaration of Independence as his sufficient answer. Here, as the House was trying Sam Houston for assaulting a fellow Member, Drayton of South Carolina declared that if freedom of discussion were ever restrained, the pillars of the Constitution would fall.

Here, in the middle of one war, Tom Corwin had the courage to proclaim that if he were a Mexican, he would welcome American invaders with bloody hands to hospitable graves; and just before our entry in another, Robert M. La Follette, Sr., halted the armed-ship bill amid a hurricane of denunciation. Here, when Andrew Johnson was placed on trial, a little knot of determined men vindicated the demands of justice and the authority of the Presidency.

We can assert that the Capitol has heard eloquence equaling that of any parliament on earth; that it has written into law such immortal charters of idealism as the Fourteenth Amendment; and that in its foreign aid bills it has enacted the most generous measures known to history. But our proudest boast is that no Capitol in the world has done more to safeguard free democratic debate, the privileges of minorities, and the fundamental civil liberties of man.

We would do an injustice to the spirit of the Capitol, however, if we emphasized merely the great men and dramatic events associated with it. The value of democratic government lies mainly in the place it gives to ordinary aspiring men and women. Since 1800 the Capitol has been the scene of grim, hard work by many thousands of conscientious legislators and their aides who have thought little of public fame, but much of the honest accomplishment of their tasks. We too often treat these servants, toiling early and late, as a matter of course.

If the stars were visible only once in a thousand years, wrote Emerson, we should await the spectacle with breathless interest; but our legislators, like the stars, are visible all the time, and hence are little noted unless of special magnitude. The Capitol is History; it is the Major Symbol of the Nation, full of minor symbols; but above all it is a Mighty Engine, tended and kept throbbing by the indefatigable efforts of a select assemblage which represents far more of our national strengths than our national weaknesses.

ALLAN NEVINS

Sharp against the skyline on a hilltop height stands the Nation's Capitol,

The Meaning of the Capitol

By LONNELLE AIKMAN

LIKE A VISION in fantasy, the great white Dome of the United States Capitol rises above the trees at the end of converging avenues in Washington. Floodlit by night or cameo-cut against azure skies, it reminds Americans of classroom prints and pledges of allegiance, of high school Civics I, commemorative stamps—and a procession of domed and columned statehouses repeating the classic national profile all across the land. No other building, not even the White House, is so intimately linked

8

citadel of democracy epitomized in Alexander Hamilton's "Here, sir, the people govern."

with the lives of all the people of the United States. It stands at the heart of our system of representative government. It is a focal point of American ideals of freedom and opportunity. It is proof—in stone, marble, and partisan debate—of the capacity of citizens to join in the adventures and satisfactions of governing themselves.

Here our elected representatives make the laws we live by, under our Constitution beginning, "We, the people . . . in order to form a more perfect Union, establish justice, . . . provide for the common defense, promote the general welfare. . . ." Here voices raised in legislative argument echo accents of 50 states. They speak of the conflicting interests of city, factory, and farm—of seaboard, plain, and mountain regions in a far-flung Nation. Then the votes are counted, and all voices merge into the majority that can speak as one for the United States.

There is a phrase for this democratic process. High above Congress, it is incised on the base of the Statue of Freedom that crowns the Dome. Taken from the Great Seal of the United States, it reads "*E Pluribus Unum*"—"Out of Many, One."

Such symbolism pervades the Capitol. It was built into the walls, stone by stone, as the "Congress House" kept pace with the expanding Nation. It is inherent in the dignity of today's structure, and in the architectural balance between the two wings.

Symbolic themes turn up, too, in structural and decorative details bequeathed by dedicated architects and artists who labored on the Capitol. From pride in New World products, for instance, came the Indian-corn and tobacco-leaf designs chosen to ornament columns in the original Senate wing.

"This Capital [the column head with the corn-ear motif]...obtained me more applause from Members of Congress," architect Benjamin Latrobe wrote President Jefferson, "than all the Works of Magnitude, of difficulty & of splendor that surround them."

Paintings and murals displayed throughout the building highlight events of the founding, expansion, and development of the United States. Statues and portraits of the men who took part in these struggles and achievements—soldiers, statesmen, scholars, and inventors—line the marble corridors and look out from the columned walls.

T O THE MILLIONS of sightseers who annually trudge the Capitol's immense distances, the whole effect is one of kaleidoscopic variety. Indeed, the panorama of so many ideas and objects might float off into abstractions or break up into fragments were it not that the exhibits, together, evoke the story of the United States as a Nation.

It is this unifying element in our past that makes the home of Congress a tangible link between the states, recalling what Abraham Lincoln termed the "mystic chords of memory" shared by all Americans. In the Civil War, when critics complained of the cost of continuing construction, Lincoln himself cited the symbol of symbols.

"If people see the Capitol going on," a caller reported his saying, "it is a sign we intend the Union shall go on."

All three branches of the Government have had close associations with the Capitol since its first small wing was completed in 1800. For 134 years it sheltered the United States Supreme Court as well as the Congress. Here most of our Presidents have been inaugurated, beginning with Thomas Jefferson, who in 1801 strolled over from his nearby boarding house to take the oath of office.

FATEFUL MOMENT *and dramatic action link Nation and history within the Capitol's marbled halls. Here statesmen tread, strong wills clash, laws pass—an atom-tinged issue today, in the past, a Compro-*

ROBERT WHITECHURCH AFTER PETER F. ROTHERMEL

mise of 1850. That event saw Henry
Clay, aged and ill, plead to the Senate
for a middle road in the North-South
split over allowing slavery's spread to
western lands. Daniel Webster
listened, head in hand, then put Union
before self to speak for the compromise
—and lost all chance at the Presidency.
Vice President Millard Fillmore presides
here, his elbow above John C. Calhoun.
William Seward glowers from the desk at
right, Thomas Hart Benton sprawls at left.

LINCOLN'S INAUGURAL *in 1861 took place beneath hoists and scaffolds of work on the Capitol Dome. Bayonets glinted as the President-elect spoke of possible civil war and reminded "dissatisfied fellow countrymen" of his oath to "preserve, protect and defend" the Constitution. Chief Justice Taney then administered that oath in a scene artist Thomas Nast sketched (below).*

Beginning with Jackson, 25 Presidents have been sworn on the Capitol's steps.

THE ILLUSTRATED NEWS, NEW YORK PUBLIC LIBRARY

Highest-ranking officials of our three-way system come together in the House Chamber whenever the Chief Executive delivers his State of the Union Message to a Joint Session of Congress, usually attended by the Justices of the Supreme Court.

More American leaders have dreamed, planned, worked, and argued in the Capitol than in any other single spot in the United States. Nineteen of our Presidents served in this building as Representatives or Senators, or both, before achieving the Nation's highest office. Two, John Quincy Adams and Andrew Johnson, returned after-

ward to the House and Senate respectively.

"My election as President...was not half so gratifying to my inmost soul," Adams confided to his diary in 1830, after winning a seat in the Twenty-second Congress.

To Johnson, his welcome back to the Senate in 1875, after the humiliation of his impeachment trial as President in that same room, was even greater balm for wounded pride. In a chamber filled with rejoicing friends and disconcerted enemies, he received congratulations and flowers, magnanimously shaking hands with men who had voted for his conviction.

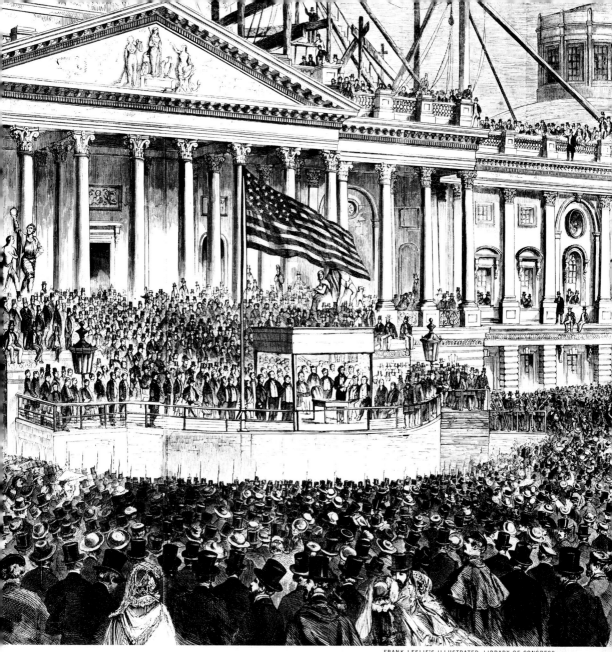

Some of the most dramatic events in our political life took place at the Capitol, beginning with the vote by the House giving Jefferson the Presidency over Aaron Burr after the electoral tie of February, 1801.

During the first 60 years, Congress fought out the "great debates" over issues that split the country: Foreign-trade restrictions and protective tariffs in the early 1800's; bank legislation of Jackson's time; slave- and free-state contests marking long shadows of the coming Civil War.

On a grieving April day in 1865, Lincoln's funeral cortege moved slowly from the White House toward the Capitol that had lately flamed with gaslight celebration over Richmond's fall. There the body remained on view in the black-draped Rotunda as mourning thousands paid their last respects.

There was Woodrow Wilson before a Joint Session of Congress, on April 2, 1917, asking for a declaration of war against Germany. "The world," he said, "must be made safe for democracy." And Franklin Delano Roosevelt, before a similar session, opening another Presidential war message with the words, "Yesterday, December 7, 1941—a date which will live in infamy...."

13

Soldiers, statesmen, poets—many others —have spoken here. On a February day in 1962, a modest, youthful man stood before Congress assembled to hear a report that would have seemed sheer lunacy not so long before. The speaker was Lt. Col. John H. Glenn, Jr.; the subject, his experience as the first American to whirl in space three times around the earth.

"We have only begun," President John F. Kennedy told Congress in his January, 1963, State of the Union Message. "Upon our achievement of greater vitality and strength . . . hang our fate and future in the world."

Ten months later an assassin's bullet had cut down America's youngest elected President. At the Capitol, his successor—former Vice President and President of the Senate Lyndon B. Johnson—voiced a pledge:

"We will continue," he said, ". . . that we may fulfill the destiny that history has set for us."

Along with crises and high moments, the Capitol witnessed the central miracle of a Nation in the making—the enactment of long-range legislation that pulled a continent together, coordinated its natural wealth, and helped root in its soil what we call the American way of life.

In fact, the departments and agencies of the Government—with but very few exceptions—have each been established through action by Congress; all owe their continued existence to the sanction of the people's representatives, whose responsibilities are reflected in the size and complexities of today's Capitol.

The building towers 287 feet 5½ inches, from East Front base to the top of the Statue of Freedom. It is 350 feet wide; more than 751 feet long. Its floor area covers 16½ acres. Its 540 rooms hum with activities of committee hearings, administrative and maintenance chores, and a thousand other operations devoted to the perennial consideration of legislation.

How this huge, labyrinthine building became the center and symbol of a Nation that did not even exist less than 200 years ago is an American success story all the more fascinating because it began under the most unlikely circumstances and in a swamp.

ROTUNDA VISITORS *mill in knots around guides or gaze at works of art in the great circular hall beneath the Capitol Dome. The 96-foot-wide room was new when a civic reception in it honored Lafayette in 1824. Later, hucksters peddled mousetraps there. Today, millions of persons pass through each year on pilgrimages to the building that stands as the heart of our system of representative government.*

PENSIVE LINCOLN *dwarfs a tiny admirer. The work of Vinnie Ream (left), the statue stands at the west entrance of the Rotunda. Lincoln let her sketch him in the White House when he learned that she was poor.*

15

A Building and a Nation Grow

NOT EVERYONE was pleased, in 1790, when Congress decided to found the young Republic's permanent seat on the banks of the Potomac River instead of accepting one of a dozen other sites offered.

"A howling, malarious, wilderness," some called the area chosen. "The Indian place...in the woods on the Potomac," said one disgusted official.

But the decision had been made, and much could be said for it. Washington, District of Columbia—marked off by, and named for, the first President—was near the mid-point of the long stretch of states. It lay close to the thriving centers of Georgetown and Alexandria, accessible to overland and water transport. "It is a beautiful spot, capable of any improvement," said Mrs. John Adams when she first saw her brief home as the wife of the second President, "...the more I view it the more I am delighted with it."

Few realized it then, but the embryo settlement also was favored by the vision of a city planner on the grand scale. Pierre Charles L'Enfant, French-born engineer who had served under General Washington in the Revolution, laid out a city whose broad avenues and sweeping circles anticipated the needs of the future metropolis.

On a June morning in 1791, President Washington and L'Enfant made a horseback inspection of the Federal District's wooded and swampy site. L'Enfant had prepared a map and report on the city's proposed features, including the home of Congress and the "presidential palace," linked by a broad green mall.

"I could discover no one [situation]," L'Enfant wrote in his report, "so advantageously to greet the congressional

PRESIDENT WASHINGTON, *wearing sash, collar, and apron of the Masonic order, lays the cornerstone for the Capitol on September 18, 1793. Dismantling in 1959 at the building's East Front—though failing to uncover the original stone—revealed that no brick went into its area, as this artist's conception shows. The marble-headed gavel and silver trowel Washington used still exist; they have figured in later stone-setting ceremonies at the Capitol, the Washington Monument, and other public structures.*

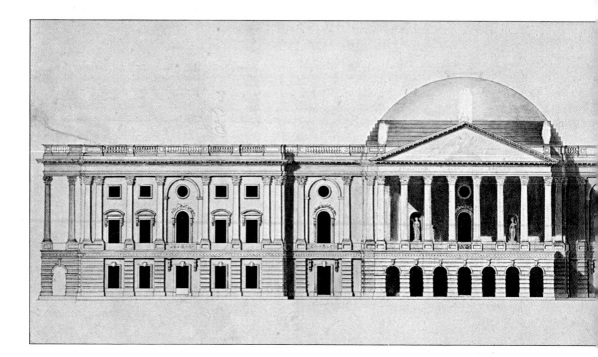

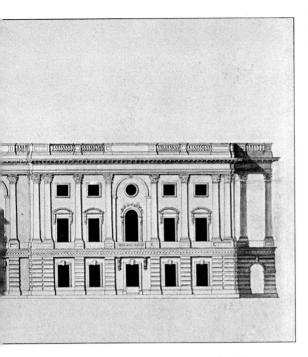

LOW-DOMED BUILDING *won for Dr. William Thornton a 1792 competition for a Capitol design. His prize: $500 and a city lot. Washington praised the plan for its "Grandeur, Simplicity and Convenience." The original drawing was lost; this is a second, slightly revised, version.*

CAPITOL DESIGN *by Stephen Hallet placed second in the contest. He was named to oversee construction on Thornton's draft, but, ambitious, sought to put in ideas from his own. Commissioners discharged him in 1794.*

OUTSIZED WEATHERCOCK *topped the Capitol building proposed by James Diamond, of Maryland. Other sketches submitted in the rivalry had equally impossible details or odd proportions; few trained architects then existed in the United States.*

WILLIAM THORNTON—*physician, painter, and inventor—turned amateur architect to enter contests for designing a library in Philadelphia and, later, the U. S. Capitol. Born in 1759 on a tiny island near Tortola in the West Indies, he studied medicine in Edinburgh, lived in Paris, and moved to the United States in 1787.*

The deadline for Capitol entries was three months past when Thornton asked permission to compete. Officials, dissatisfied with drawings already received, granted it. The plan that resulted "captivated the eyes and judgment of all," Secretary of State Thomas Jefferson commented.

As architect in the Capitol's construction until 1802, Thornton clashed with Hallet and others associated with the project who had more formal training. He became head of the Patent Office —a story credits his pleas to a British officer with saving that building from being burned in the War of 1812.

Thornton died in 1828.

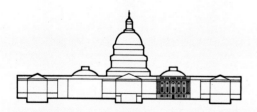

BOXLIKE WING *of the old Capitol, first to be completed, served Senate, House, and Supreme Court. This water color was done in 1800. Small sketch shows the wing's location in today's building. Sandstone, chosen by George Washington for economy, came from a Virginia quarry.*

building as is that on the west end of Jenkins heights. . . ." It stands, he added in the felicitous, oft-quoted phrase, "as a pedestal waiting for a monument."

To obtain a suitable design for their monument, the District Commissioners announced a Capitol competition, offering the winner $500 and a city lot. The contest was advertised in newspapers of the young country where professional architects were few, but none of the entries proved satisfactory. Some—notably one showing a giant wingspread weathervane apparently crowing from the rooftop—were ludicrous.

At this crucial moment, a versatile young man named William Thornton (physician, portrait painter, steamboat experimenter, and amateur architect) gained permission to submit a belated design.

When his plan arrived, it "captivated the eyes and judgment of all," said another tal-

ented amateur architect—Thomas Jefferson, then Secretary of State.

"Grandeur, Simplicity and Convenience appear to be so well combined in this plan . . ." George Washington wrote in a letter of recommendation to the District Commissioners, "that I have no doubt of its meeting with . . . approbation from you."

By September 18, 1793, Dr. Thornton's design for a stately building with two wings joined by a domed center had been selected and modified. Troublesome construction problems had been resolved, and the time had come to lay the Capitol's cornerstone.

The day's program involved elaborate Masonic ceremonies, a common practice then, with roots going back to the link between medieval stonemasons and the order. As President, war hero, and Acting Grand Master of Maryland's Grand Lodge, Washington had the lead role, supported by a uniformed and decorated cast from the Alexandria Volunteer Artillery and Masonic lodges of Maryland, Virginia, and the District. A parade began with the President's

SLOOPS EDGE *Philadelphia wharves as the Government moves to Washington from its last temporary capital in 1800.*

WILLIAM R. BIRCH, LIBRARY OF CONGRESS; JOSEPH E. BARRETT (BELOW)

MASONIC SYMBOLS *chiseled by members of the craft who cut the stone still show under stairs in the Old House wing.*

arrival on the Virginia shore of the "Grand River Patowmack," crossed to the Maryland side, and moved on to the President's Square, collecting additions at each meeting place.

"The procession marched two abreast," an observer reported in the September 25th issue of the Alexandria *Gazette,* "in the greatest solemn dignity, with music playing, drums beating, colours flying and spectators rejoicing."

Skirting the "great Serbonian Bog" that was then Pennsylvania Avenue, the marchers followed a new post road, broke ranks to step from stone to stone or to teeter over a single log across Tiber Creek at the foot of Capitol Hill, and proceeded to the hilltop building site.

There, Washington, wearing a Masonic apron reportedly "the handiwork of Mrs. General La Fayette" and wielding a silver trowel and marble-headed gavel, laid the cornerstone. On it he placed an engraved silver plate marking the date as the 13th year of American independence, the first year of his second term, and the year of Masonry 5793. The cornerstone's exact site today remains uncertain, though it may be in the southeast corner area of the Capitol's original north wing.

"The ceremony ended in prayer, Masonic chanting Honours, and a fifteen volley from the Artillery," the Alexandria *Gazette* told readers. "The whole company retired to an extensive booth, where an ox of 500 pounds' weight was barbequed, of which the company generally partook,

JAMES HOBAN *gained a footnote in history by his prize-winning plans for the "President's Palace"—the White House—in 1792. But he also had a part in shaping the Capitol. Born in Ireland in 1758, he trained as an artisan and architect and emigrated to the United States after the Revolution. He lived in South Carolina and designed, among other buildings, the State House, burned during the Civil War. Winning the White House contest brought Hoban an appointment to superintend construction. A year later the Capitol became his responsibility, too. With but one interlude, he held the position until 1802, though his assistant Stephen Hallet for a time took rather free rein. Hoban was active in Government building until his death in 1831.*

LEWIS AND CLARK, *on $2,500 voted by Congress, made an 1804-6 journey to the Pacific that revealed the West's dazzling promise. This print of the explorers meeting with Indians came from an 1810 account of the trek.*

LOUISIANA PURCHASE *in 1803 nearly doubled the Nation's size. Bought from France for $15,000,000—2½ cents an acre—on Jefferson's initiative, it won Congress' approval after debate over whether the Constitution was violated.*

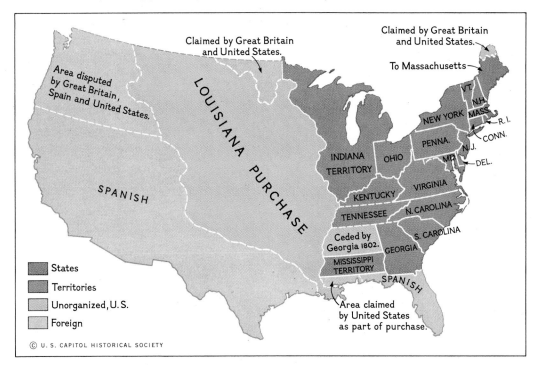

Claimed by Great Britain and United States.

Claimed by Great Britain and United States.

To Massachusetts

Area disputed by Great Britain, Spain and United States.

LOUISIANA PURCHASE

SPANISH

VT
N.H.
NEW YORK MASS.
R. I.
CONN.
PENNA.
N.J.
INDIANA TERRITORY OHIO MD. DEL.
VIRGINIA
KENTUCKY
TENNESSEE N.CAROLINA
Ceded by Georgia 1802. S. CAROLINA
GEORGIA
MISSISSIPPI TERRITORY
SPANISH

Area claimed by United States as part of purchase.

■ States
■ Territories
□ Unorganized, U.S.
□ Foreign

ⓒ U. S. CAPITOL HISTORICAL SOCIETY

BENJAMIN HENRY LATROBE *took
over construction of the Capitol
on his appointment as Surveyor
of Public Buildings in 1803. An
English architect, he was born in
1764 and came to the United States
in 1796. The Capitol's exterior
design was already set, so he poured
out his genius on the interior.
Hiring sculptors from abroad, he put
them to work executing ideas that
won acclaim, including corn and
tobacco motifs on columns (below).
Latrobe had the task of repairing
the British-burned Capitol, resigning
after a dispute in 1817.
He died in 1820.*

with every abundance of other recreation."

It was a brave beginning, but troubles were already brewing.

One of the difficulties was the rivalry between Dr. Thornton, the official architect of the Capitol, and a series of professional architects who wished to alter the prize-winning design.

Etienne Sulpice Hallet, or Stephen Hallet, as Americans simplified the French name, was the first to come to grief over this issue. Hallet's disappointment in having been rated second best in the original competition complicated the conflict. By the end of 1794, Hallet—in charge of construction at the Capitol—had been dismissed, and Thornton promoted to be one of the three District Commissioners, with over-all authority to back up his own ideas.

MEANTIME, the meager sale of lots in the straggling village could not finance the public buildings, as had been hoped. The Commissioners were forced to borrow money on loans guaranteed by Congress. Skilled workmen, tools, and materials needed to build the Capitol proved hard to get.

Yet somehow the Congress House progressed. The first, or north, wing was completed under the general direction of the superintendent of construction, James Hoban, who designed and also directed the building of the "President's Palace"—the White House. Except for details, the wing was ready to receive the legislators by the autumn of 1800, when the Government had moved, bag and baggage, from its last temporary seat at Philadelphia.

In the columned Senate Chamber, under the intent gaze of spectators, President John Adams addressed the first Joint Session in the building on November 22, 1800. He wore the formal coat, knee breeches, and powdered hair of the time, and his words reflected the importance of the occasion. Not until Woodrow Wilson in 1913 did another President appear in person to address Congress.

"I congratulate the people of the United States on the assembling of Congress at the permanent seat of their government," Adams said, "and I congratulate you, gentlemen, on the prospect of a residence not

to be changed.... May this Territory be the residence of virtue and happiness! In this city may that piety and virtue, that wisdom and magnanimity, that constancy and self-government, which adorned the great character whose name it bears, be forever held in veneration!"

Both the congratulations and the hopes must have echoed hollowly to the lawmakers as they prepared to settle down in the near-wilderness of the District of Columbia during that first winter of 1800.

"I do not perceive," Secretary of the Treasury Oliver Wolcott wrote his wife in Connecticut, "how the members of Congress can possibly secure lodgings, unless they will consent to live like Scholars in a college or Monks in a monastery, crowded ten or twenty in one house, and utterly secluded from Society."

The situation was hardly better at the Capitol itself, where the 32-member Senate,

WOODEN WALKWAY *connected House and Senate wings before British soldiers fired the Capitol in 1814. Latrobe made this water color from memory later. Indians once had a council chamber at the foot of the Capitol's hill. Tinted part of the small sketch shows the House wing occupied in 1807 and its location now (West Front view).*

25

106-man House, Supreme Court, Circuit Court, and Library of Congress would soon share one modest rectangular building.

Officials and clerks, however, could already see hope for expansion in the partially laid foundations of the Capitol's central section and south wing protruding from the barren, stone-cluttered hilltop. And soon began a game of musical chairs, played by these august branches of Government as they exchanged old quarters for new in a forever changing and growing building.

The Representatives moved first (1801), into a one-story, oval-shaped hall—appropriately nicknamed the "Oven"—erected temporarily on the south-wing site. The Oven was razed in 1804, and House members returned to their earlier quarters on the west side of the north wing. There they met for three more years while their own chamber rose where the Oven had stood.

The architect now in charge of the Capitol was Benjamin Henry Latrobe, appointed by President Jefferson in 1803.

As had Washington, Jefferson took a keen personal interest in the building's development, even to dictating many of its details. He particularly admired Latrobe's

SHOUTING HEADLINES in Boston's Columbian Centinel of June 24, 1812, announce the step urged on Congress by fiery young "War Hawks" in its ranks. They called war "the only means of redress" for interference with American trade, impressment of American seamen, and other acts by Great Britain. At the war's end, the Capitol where they spoke lay in ruins.

finished House Chamber, with its carvings, classical columns, and visitors' gallery.

"I declared on many and all occasions," he wrote Latrobe, "that I considered you as the only person in the United States who could have executed the ... Chamber. ..."

UNFORTUNATELY, though all agreed that the new room was magnificent in appearance, its acoustics proved far from satisfactory. Virginia Representative John Randolph of Roanoke summed up the verdict when he called it "handsome and fit for anything but the use intended."

While the House hung red-baize draperies behind Corinthian columns in an effort to muffle resounding echoes, the Senate grappled with its own brand of construction and moving-day problems.

Besides stopping leaks and patching cracks that threatened the north wing with premature decay, Latrobe raised the floor part way up the two-story chamber in which the Senate had met since 1800, thus creating two separate rooms.

During the renovation, displaced Senators occupied quarters on the wing's west side; then in January, 1810, took over the

"BATTLE OF LAKE ERIE," *a painting by William H. Powell, hangs in the east stairway of the Senate wing. It depicts 28-year-old Oliver Hazard Perry transferring the colors from his battered flagship, the* Lawrence, *to the* Niagara *in the 1813 engagement. Vandals once slashed a corner of the canvas, completed in 1871, but restorers skillfully repaired the cut.*

BRITISH TROOPS, *ordered to "destroy and lay waste," set fire to public buildings in Washington, August 24, 1814. The act incensed Americans, shamed many Britons. "Cossacks spared Paris, but we spared not the Capitol of America," one newspaper said. This sketch appeared in London in 1815.*

REAR ADM. SIR GEORGE COCKBURN *took part in firing the Capitol. Reportedly, he stood on the House Speaker's chair, asked "Shall this harbor of Yankee democracy be burned?"*

BURNED-OUT CAPITOL *stood stark after a rainstorm checked the flames. Piled furniture, books from the Library of Congress, and tar barrels made tinder for the blaze. Latrobe replaced gutted wood of the interior with marble, brick, and metal.*

TREASURY REPORT *survived the fire. Handwriting on its flyleaf says Admiral Cockburn took it from the Capitol and gave it to his brother. A dealer presented it to the Library of Congress in 1940.*

PIERRE MION (ABOVE), AND THE NATIONAL CAPITOL, LIBRARY OF CONGRESS

MONROE'S INAUGURAL
outdoors settled a dispute over whether to sit on the Senate's "fine red chairs" or the "plain democratic" ones of the House. His open-air oath-taking—later a tradition—occurred at the "Brick Capitol" (left). The building housed Congress during 1815-19 repairs to the burned quarters. A prison during the Civil War, it stood where the Supreme Court Building now is.

top part of their old chamber. In turn the Supreme Court, then made up of seven members, transferred its sessions to the ground-floor level.

Presiding was Chief Justice John Marshall, whose long, brilliant career would build the Court's prestige as arbiter of the Constitution, and lay a firm legal foundation for legislative powers of Congress.

Hardly a dozen years had passed since the Government's move to Washington, but already its leaders could look back on some notable accomplishments. They had built two wings of a Capitol planned to accommodate more than 500 future lawmakers. And they had made enough national history there to indicate that the building's scope was not excessive.

In 1803 Congress ratified Jefferson's vast Louisiana Purchase—though not without lively discussion as to whether it violated the Constitution. It voted funds for the Lewis and Clark Expedition that revealed a new world of dazzling promise and sobering responsibility to men struggling in Washington to unify a string of independent-minded coastal states. And it appropriated money to strengthen the infant United States Navy for action against Barbary pirates preying on Mediterranean shipping.

Then came a day in November, 1805, when a mission from the Bey of Tunis arrived in the village by the Potomac. As a courtesy, the Senate received the Tunisian Ambassador in its Chamber, where that turbaned envoy expressed bewilderment at the spectacle of ordinary men being allowed to speak at length on the conduct of their Government.

Less picturesque, but no less significant as a promise of things to come, was the establishment by Congress, in the early 1800's, of a reference library. Out of the first $5,000 provided to stock the Capitol's one-room Library of Congress would come a world-renowned institution that now occupies two huge buildings and contains more than fifty million books, manuscripts, periodicals, dramas, and works of music and art.

"There is no subject to which a Member of Congress may not have occasion to refer," Jefferson said in an observation even more applicable today.

But first the young Republic faced the War of 1812, and ordeal by fire to determine whether either Capitol or Library, or the Nation itself, would have a future.

Congress declared war against Great Britain on June 18, 1812, after long and bitter debates between "War Hawks" and peace proponents over neutral rights, British impressment of American seamen, western lands, and other issues creating bad feeling between the two countries.

For many months after fighting began, most of the action took place far from Washington. Then, in the late summer of 1814, a British squadron under Rear Adm. Sir George Cockburn landed soldiers and marines near Benedict on Maryland's Patuxent shore. Brushing aside American forces hurriedly gathered at Bladensburg, the invaders captured Washington on August 24, and set fire to most of its public buildings.

INDIGNANT PATRIOTS later claimed that Admiral Cockburn himself led a detachment of troops into the House Chamber. They said he took over the Speaker's chair and put the rhetorical question, "Shall this harbor of Yankee democracy be burned?" The motion carried with a roar of "ayes."

The men ignited piles of flammable materials—chairs, desks, and books—in both House and Senate wings. Interiors were gutted, exteriors scarred and blackened, and the wooden passageway between the two buildings destroyed.

Destruction would probably have been total, except for a rainstorm that swept the city that night. The next day brought a violent windstorm. Its force destroyed houses, killed 30 British soldiers, and blew cannon off their mounts. Together with an accidental gunpowder explosion and a false rumor that American troops were gathering to retake Washington, the chain of disasters so shook British confidence that the redcoats moved out, never to return.

Amid the clamor of Members demanding the Government's transfer to another city, the homeless Congress met that fall in the Patent Office Building, formerly Sam Blodget's hotel—the only Government office structure to escape burning.

From late 1815 to 1819, Congressional

sessions were held in a new building hastily erected by a group of private citizens and rented cheaply to Congress as an inducement to stay on. This building, long known as the Brick Capitol, stood on the site of what is now the United States Supreme Court Building. There, on March 4, 1817, James Monroe took the Presidential oath in Washington's first outdoor inaugural.

The ceremony—"grand, animating and impressive"—was the result of a deadlock between spokesmen for the two legislative bodies on the question of whether to sit on the "fine red chairs" from the Senate or the "plain democratic chairs" of the House.

Rebuilding the Capitol, meanwhile, proceeded under the direction of architect Latrobe, who had spent the war years away on projects ranging from designing Mississippi steamboats to planning waterworks for New Orleans.

On his recall in 1815, Latrobe found "the devastation . . . dreadful. . . . a most magnificent ruin." Setting resolutely to work, he strengthened as well as restored both wings, using sandstone and marble, brick and metal. He enlarged and beautified the Senate Chamber, and redesigned the House Chamber into the semicircular shape we see today as Statuary Hall.

SCARLET CURTAINS *in the Old House Chamber hung as much for utility as for decoration—to muffle annoying echoes. Samuel F. B. Morse painted this night session of the House in 1822. Visitors now see the area as Statuary Hall.*

Done before Morse turned from easel to telegraph experiments, the painting shows an attendant lighting the lowered chandelier. In 1847 gas lamps came, electricity in 1885. Morse faithfully reproduced House details, recorded Members' likenesses by individual sittings.

LAFAYETTE'S PORTRAIT, *a gift by its French painter, Ary Scheffer, has hung in the House since 1825.*

But Latrobe, too, suffered from the occupational hazard of Capitol architects—disagreement with his boss, the Commissioner of Public Buildings. He resigned in 1817 to make way for able Boston architect Charles Bulfinch, the first American-born citizen to receive the appointment.

To Bulfinch goes the credit for completing the Capitol as Thornton and Latrobe planned it. He worked out remaining structural details of Senate and House Chambers in time for Congress to move back on December 6, 1819. And he carried through the building's long-planned central portion, including its east and west fronts, and a

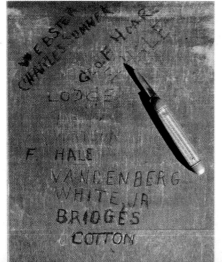

DANIEL WEBSTER'S REPLY *to Senator Hayne (next to solon with curls) boomed a "Liberty and Union, now and forever, one and inseparable!" thesis to the Southerner's stand for states' rights. The date: 1830. G. P. A. Healy's painting hangs in Boston's Faneuil Hall.*

NAMES CARVED *in a drawer of Webster's desk note other Senators who have occupied the great orator's seat.*

34

central Rotunda covered by a low copper-sheathed dome.

The cornerstone for the Capitol's center section was laid on August 24, 1818, four years to the day after the British bonfire. By October, 1824, the Rotunda was far enough along to be opened for a gala civic reception to honor a visiting dignitary and old friend—the Marquis de Lafayette. Fashionable Washington—eager to shake the hand of the French general and statesman who had helped create the Nation—jammed the great circular hall.

In December Congress officially received the Revolutionary hero, making him the first foreign visitor to speak before a Joint Meeting. Lafayette was aging now, but with charm undiminished by the years. To a remark made by Henry Clay, Speaker of the House, that he stood "in the midst of posterity," he replied that, on the contrary, he stood in the midst of his friends.

From the 1820's to the eve of Civil War, the Capitol was the stage for momentous and tragic events—sometimes for scenes not far from comic opera. It was the era of

BULFINCH'S DOME *and Capitol addition gave Congress' home this look from 1825-56. City planner L'Enfant called its hill site "a pedestal waiting for a monument."*

leisurely oratory, filled with learned classical allusions, and on occasion with barbed insults that led Congressional opponents to uphold their honor on the dueling field.

It was an age of chivalry, when the gentlemen of the House and Senate welcomed visiting ladies to the floors of their respective halls, or, seeing their guests sitting for hours in hot and crowded galleries, would pass up refreshments of fruit tied to the ends of long sticks.

But most of all it was a time of struggle and dissension, a period when sectional rivalries strained the bonds between the states and the national Government.

The arena of test and decision was the United States Congress. Here opposing lead-

ers wooed followers and votes in verbal combats on such crucial subjects as the tariff, states' rights, and conflicting interests of West, South, and North.

Within this same short time span, the Capitol also saw much to nourish Americans' increasing sense of national pride and "manifest destiny." In 1823, Congress heard the bold Monroe Doctrine proclaimed, warning Europe's rulers against intervention in this hemisphere. Congress voted for annexation of Texas in 1845, and the next year for war with Mexico and a treaty with Great Britain to settle the dispute over the far Northwest. By the end of 1848, these events had brought the Southwest, California, and Oregon Territory under the United States

CHARLES BULFINCH *became the first native-American architect to have charge of construction at the Capitol. Boston-born in 1763, he had a Harvard education, followed by years of practical experience in building construction and wide study of architecture abroad. When Latrobe resigned in 1817, Bulfinch received the appointment to succeed him on work at the Capitol.*

There the able Bostonian mainly carried out plans set down by predecessors, although he did modify Latrobe's grandiose design for the West Front into the more pleasing lines it has today. To him goes the credit for completing the Capitol much as Thornton had envisioned it.

Bulfinch left Washington in 1830, a year after his position as architect was abolished. Not until 1851 was there a successor—or need for one except on a temporary basis. Bulfinch died in 1844.

flag. That year, as a bonus, gold was discovered in California.

Now the sectional question hung heavy with threat. In the North-South battle to extend or block the spread of slavery to the West, which side would win? Or would both lose in the breakup of the Union?

For four decades the divisive rivalry called into play the talents and energies of some of the most dynamic men who ever sat in the Congress. Three stood out as giants.

Spellbinder Henry Clay of Kentucky won his brightest laurels for his role in slavery-compromise bills of 1820 and 1850 that gave the South a temporary middle ground between secession and submission—and the North years of economic and population growth that made victory possible in the fratricidal war.

John C. Calhoun, of South Carolina, fought more often against Clay than with him, and ended his career with a tragic plea for concessions from the North. Yet by his parliamentary genius, mastery of logic, and personal integrity, this champion of rights of a minority earned the permanent respect of his country as well as of his section.

Last of the triumvirate was Daniel Web-

COLONNADED WALLS *of the Old Senate Chamber once resounded to orations by such as Calhoun, Clay, and Webster. And, in lighter moments, gentlemen on the Chamber floor passed refreshments up by stick to friends in the stuffy galleries. After the Senate moved into its present wing in 1859, the room for 75 years housed the Supreme Court.*

Here the hall looks as it appeared in 1842. Engraver Thomas Doney made the mezzotint by peopling gallery seats and desks with individual daguerreotypes of Senators and other noted persons.

The galleries came down when the Chamber was converted for use by the Court. Desks went into the new Senate quarters, where many still are in use. Others added are copies of the original mahogany ones made by a New York cabinetmaker in 1819.

The gilded eagle (above) still perches on a Chamber wall.

ster of Massachusetts. The most compelling orator America has produced, he poured his heart and thunderous eloquence into the struggle to preserve the Union. In his "Seventh of March" speech, he dramatically pleaded for Senate passage of Clay's 1850 compromise—but at high cost to the man. By daring to repudiate not only his Free Soil followers, but his own pledge to oppose extension of slavery—in any place, at any time—Webster was denounced by friends and lost his last chance of winning enough support to achieve his greatest ambition, the Presidency.

Throughout the long tumult, states continued to join the Union, population soared, and Congress grew. In 1850, the 62 Senators and 232 Representatives were beginning to feel crowded. Ironically, the drive for more space was spearheaded by Senator Jefferson Davis, whose later fame as President of the Confederate States has overshadowed his earlier career.

Congress in September, 1850, appropriated $100,000 to begin work on "ample accommodations for the two houses of Congress," an enlargement that reduced the Capitol's original wings to the role of links

between the additions and central Rotunda. President Millard Fillmore, authorized to select both design and architect, took features from several drawings and appointed Thomas U. Walter of Philadelphia to draw up the final plans.

The building's third cornerstone laying took place on July 4, 1851. It was an unqualified success, free "from all untoward occurrences," reported Washington's popular newspaper, the *National Intelligencer.* "The day was ushered in by salutes of artillery from different points of the city, and as the glorious sun gilded our tallest spires, and shed a lustre on the dome of the Capitol, it was welcomed by a display of National Flags and the ringing of bells from the various churches and engine houses."

President Fillmore and the Grand Master of the Masonic fraternity, B. B. French, laid the stone in elaborate civil and Masonic ceremonies. But the chief event for which the crowd had gathered from far and near was the dedication address by the old master, Daniel Webster, now Secretary of State.

The most frequently quoted paragraph from Webster's two-hour speech was also part of his own handwritten statement buried inside the cornerstone with other mementos of the proceedings.

"If therefore," his deep, melodic voice rang out over the Capitol's stilled east plaza, "it shall be hereafter the will of God that this structure shall fall from its base, that its foundation be upturned, and this deposit brought to the eyes of men, be it then known that, on this day, the Union of the United States stands firm; that their constitution still exists unimpaired, and with all its original usefulness and glory. . . ."

Work on the massive additions for the Capitol went forward as fast as possible, but architect Walter faced many problems, including the usual conflicts over authority, trouble in obtaining materials, and a fire in 1851 that made it necessary to reconstruct the area housing the Library of Congress.

NEITHER WING was fully completed when House and Senate moved in, the House for its first session in the new south building December 16, 1857, and the Senate in the northern side January 4, 1859. The legislative halls were models of beauty, with paneled walls, arabesque decorations, and intricate glass-and-iron skylights. The spacious chambers even had newfangled gas lighting; the House briefly tried luxurious settees as a substitute for desks.

Indeed, considering the existing political situation, there was something decidedly incongruous about the lavishness of the Capitol's latest accommodations and plans for the future.

As the 1850's closed, the clash of wills in Congress reflected the country's rising tensions. Abolitionists and slavery diehards jammed the shiny new galleries, tossing out leaflets and hissing or cheering the impassioned speakers.

"Every man on the floor of both Houses is armed with a revolver," observed Sena-

MORSE'S TELEGRAPH *taps its historic "What hath God wrought!" from the Supreme Court Chamber, May 24, 1844. Annie Ellsworth gives the inventor the message to be sent—a privilege earned when she brought him word, a year earlier, that Congress had voted funds to build a line from Washington to Baltimore. Witnesses to its test included Henry Clay, standing by Dolley Madison in the background.*

The Smithsonian Institution owns this key (right) used by Morse.

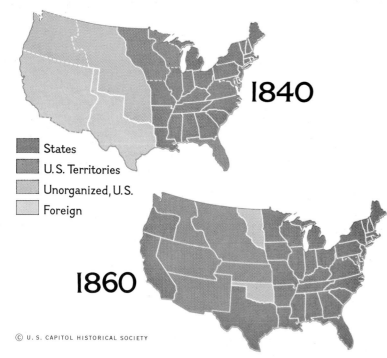

1840

States
U.S. Territories
Unorganized, U.S.
Foreign

1860

EXPLODING GROWTH
*saw the Nation fulfill a
"manifest destiny" to
stretch from sea to sea.
Population nearly doubled
—to 31 million—between
1840 and 1860. With it
came heady tales of easy
wealth and ample land.
Men dared dusty plain and
lofty mountain. And they
spread across the 1.2
million square miles
added by events linked
to Texas, the Mexican
War, and the Northwest
boundary dispute.*

PIONEERS STRUGGLE *across a rugged divide in this mural at the west staircase of the House wing. Titled "Westward the Course of Empire Takes Its Way," it was painted by Emanuel Leutze in 1862.*

Plains from Wyoming to New Mexico still show ruts cut by lurching wagons as waves of immigrants rolled west. They followed the lure of land and gold, and they peopled a burgeoning nation.

TROUBLES GROW *as expansion fans free-soil and slave-state rivalries. Border raids, such as this sack of Osawatomie, Kansas, John Brown's home, set a stage for the Civil War.*

SOLDIERS LOLL *in the Rotunda in 1861. The Capitol served as barracks in the early months of the war, then as a hospital for battle wounded. Men called their quarters the "Big Tent." Here canvas shields Rotunda paintings; a scaffold rises for construction of the Dome.*

tor James H. Hammond of South Carolina. When one member accidentally dropped his weapon during a bitter eight-week struggle to elect a Speaker of the House, the uproar threatened to turn into mob violence.

Yet when secession came, and the Southerners, one by one, bade their colleagues goodbye, the scenes were often stiff with dignity and poignant with pent-up emotion. No speech was more dramatic than the appeal to his colleagues, on January 10, 1861, by the Senator from Mississippi— gaunt, courtly Jefferson Davis.

Like Calhoun, Davis pleaded for peace. He had tried to avert war, he told the Senators and presiding officer, Vice President Breckinridge of Kentucky, who also would soon join the Confederate side. But if peace was not to be, said Davis, "then Mississippi's gallant sons will stand like a wall of fire

CAPITOL VAULTS *became storehouses for flour, beef, and pork when Washington feared siege at the war's onset. From stockpiles in arched passages, barrels skidded down planked steps to improvised bakeries. Basement committee rooms, bricked into ovens, made bread for Army forts and batteries ringing the city.*

47

HOISTED COLUMN.
swings into place outside the corridor linking old and new House wings. Men at right of the pillar probably are Jefferson Davis, a Mississippi Senator when this 1860 photograph was made, and Thomas U. Walter, Capitol architect.

CANVAS PROTECTS
men dressing columns. House wing lacks porticoes finished in 1867.

TIERED DOME *rises atop the Capitol during Civil War years. Lincoln called construction "a sign we intend the Union shall go on." Twin-shelled iron Dome, weighing 9 million pounds, replaced Bulfinch structure dismantled in the photograph at left. Ingenious tower built inside the Dome helped lift pieces into place from Capitol grounds.*

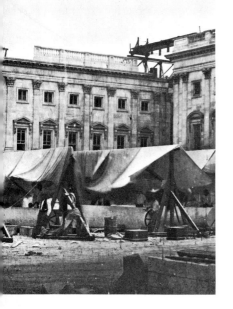

CART-SLUNG COLUMN *of iron, one of 36 in the Dome, arrives for placement. Maryland marble went into the Capitol extension's 100 other pillars—each cut from a single block of stone.*

49

DOME AND WINGS *added to the Capitol in the 1850's and 1860's brought the structure to the form so familiar today. This 1871 lithograph, hand colored, pictures it dominating a tree-dotted city from atop Jenkins Hill. The Washington Monument, incorrectly shown with capstone and round base, actually was not completed until 1884.*

around their State; and I go hence, not in hostility to you, but in love and allegiance to her...."

In the gallery sat Davis' beautiful dark-haired wife, Varina. "We felt blood in the air," she wrote later, "and mourned in secret over the severance of tender ties both of relationship and friendship ... we could even guess at the end."

Southbound Congressmen were well on their way home when President-elect Lincoln arrived, early and unannounced, in the Washington railway station on February 23. The curtain was rising on the most fateful years the Nation had yet faced.

At the Capitol on Inauguration Day, a tall, gangling figure stood on the wind-raked stand built over the East Front steps. There had been rumors of a plot to blow up the platform. Riflemen watched from the windows behind the speaker. Below him glinted the fixed bayonets of a line of soldiers.

Adjusting his steel-rimmed spectacles, Lincoln looked out on a sea of faces, not all friendly, since Washington was filled with Southern sympathizers. To these people, and those in the South, Lincoln addressed his famous appeal for conciliation:

"In *your* hands, my dissatisfied fellow countrymen, and not in *mine,* is the momentous issue of civil war.... We are not enemies, but friends. We must not be enemies. Though passion may have strained, it must not break our bonds of affection."

But there was no lack of firmness in Lincoln's inaugural speech to encourage hope that any compromise with secession was possible. "I hold," he said, "that in contemplation of universal law, and of the Constitution, the Union of these States is perpetual...no State, upon its own mere motion, can lawfully get out of the Union .... The power confided to me, will be used to hold, occupy, and possess the property,

THOMAS USTICK WALTER *guided construction during one of the Capitol's most important periods of change. Named Architect of the Capitol Extension by President Fillmore in 1851, he served until 1865—eventful years that saw the building grow almost threefold.*

Walter's father and grandfather were masons, and the Philadelphia-born youth himself became a master bricklayer while studying in an architect's office. He set up shop for himself in 1830. When a contest for enlarging the Capitol opened in 1850, Walter entered.

Four designs won acceptance; parts of each were adapted for the final plans. Named to execute them, Walter had many problems— including conflicts over authority. The Dome he built is considered a notable engineering feat.

Born in 1804, he died in 1887. His portrait by Francisco Pausas, based on a Mathew Brady photograph, shows him as Capitol architect.

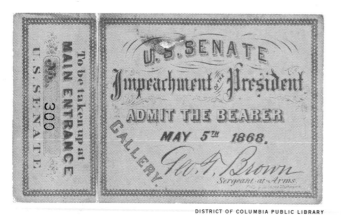

COVETED TICKET — *the Senate gallery had fewer than 800 seats — brought admission to the 1868 impeachment trial of President Andrew Johnson. Colors changed for different days of the trial.*

CROWDED SENATE CHAMBER *hears Thaddeus Stevens read the House message of impeachment. Stevens led the attempt to punish Johnson for his opposition to Congress. Sitting as a court, the Senate failed by a single vote to convict. Had impeachment succeeded, the Constitution's system of checks and balances might have given way to a parliamentary type of government.*

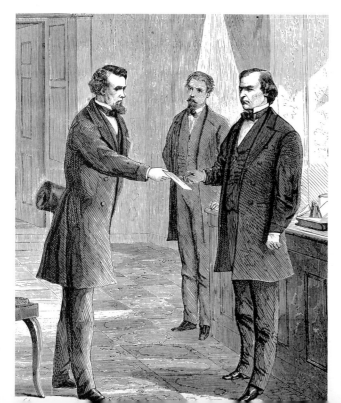

PRESIDENT JOHNSON, *at his desk in the White House, receives impeachment summons from the Senate Sergeant at Arms. As did Lincoln, Johnson favored leniency toward the South; he irked Congress by vetoing harsh Reconstruction measures.*

CARRIED IN A CHAIR, *Thaddeus Stevens enters the Capitol during the impeachment trial. Contemporary accounts called him "an infirm old man ... upheld only by an iron will." He died a few months later.*

52

HARPER'S WEEKLY (LOWER LEFT) AND FRANK LESLIE'S ILLUSTRATED, LIBRARY OF CONGRESS

and places belonging to the Government."

A month and eight days later, Confederate guns fired on Fort Sumter. For the rest of the war, the Capitol at Washington would be the Union's stronghold and symbol. The "Old Brick Capitol," across the way, would become a prison, housing for a while two famed Confederate spies, seductive Rose Greenhow and spirited Belle Boyd.

Congress was not in session when war broke. Immediately the War Department took over the marble spaces of the newly enlarged Capitol as barracks for Northern regiments marching into the city on the President's call for 75,000 state militia. The boys termed their quarters the "Big Tent," and boasted of portrait-hung parlors, comfortable sofas, and desks for writing letters home. For a time 3,000 soldiers slept in the

building, from the Rotunda and legislative chambers to hall niches and airy nooks up near the unfinished, open Dome. Mealtime found lines of hungry men waiting to cook rations of bacon, biscuits, and coffee at furnaces lighted in the basement.

The furnaces sparked an idea. Basement committee rooms were converted into a bakery that included room-sized ovens lined with fire bricks. Flour was commandeered from the city's mills. The aroma of fresh-baked bread drifted about the Capitol as Army bakers turned out enough loaves to feed even soldiers in forts and batteries springing up around Washington.

By the next autumn the cheerful bustle and youthful high jinks of what had been romantically pictured as a short, gallant war had given way to harsher realities. The Capitol, like lesser buildings, became an emergency hospital. Set up in its historic halls, chambers, and Rotunda were 1,500 cots, on which lay the sick and wounded streaming back from the battlefields of Second Manassas and Antietam.

Among the city's doctors—and a sprinkling of nurses stirred by the example of Dorothea Dix and America's future Red Cross founder, Clara Barton—moved a gentle, bearded man. Walt Whitman, poet and humanitarian, spent most of his spare time during the war in Army hospitals, dispensing small gifts and large doses of cheer.

"The hurt and wounded I pacify with soothing hand," he would write later in a poem of remembrance. "I sit by the restless all the dark night, some are so young."

With the return of Congress, following the patients' transfer to other hospitals, the Capitol became the sounding board of fears and suspicions that fevered the air of the nerve-wracked city. Accusations and denials rang out in legislative chambers. A Joint Committee on the Conduct of the War probed charges of incompetence and conspiracy. Not even the President's home escaped the pointing finger. Mary Lincoln was a spy in the White House, whispered the gossips, seeking to protect her relatives fighting on the side of the Confederates.

One morning at a secret session of investigating Senators, the towering figure of Abraham Lincoln suddenly appeared at the committee table. One of those present recalled years after that Lincoln's eyes were filled with "an almost unhuman sadness."

The President told the astonished group that he had come of his own volition, "to say that I, of my own knowledge, know that it is untrue that any of my family holds treasonable communication with the enemy."

"By tacit consent, no word being spoken," the narrator of the incident reported, "the committee dropped all consideration of the rumors that the wife of the President was betraying the Union."

DESPITE THE WAR, some work was done on the Capitol extension. Construction of a vastly enlarged Dome—authorized by Congress in 1855 to replace the one dwarfed by the new wings—continued.

Designed by architect Walter, the big Dome is a masterpiece of 19th-century engineering skill. It has outer and inner cast-iron shells, trussed to withstand the strains of contraction and expansion. Intricately girded and bolted together, it weighs nearly nine million pounds. Between the shells winds a narrow staircase of 183 steps.

To raise the heavy iron parts to their lofty places, construction superintendent M. C. Meigs built a scaffold tower up through the Dome from the floor of the Rotunda. It served as a base for the hoisting devices used to lift the materials on the outside.

The great bronze goddess that crowns the Dome's lantern structure was the work of an outstanding American sculptor, Thomas Crawford. He called her "Armed Liberty," and shaped her as a classically robed woman with one hand on a sword, the other holding a wreath and resting on a shield.

Her feathered headdress has led many to believe that the Capitol's topmost decoration represents Pocahontas or some other Indian figure. Actually, Crawford had designed the headdress as a liberty cap after those worn by Rome's emancipated slaves. He substituted a helmet with eagle head and feathers to meet the objections of Jefferson Davis, future president of the Confederacy who at that time had charge of Capitol construction as Secretary of War.

Modeled in Crawford's Rome studio, the statue's plaster cast was imperiled by a

OLD LIBRARY OF CONGRESS *quarters in the Capitol abound with ornate metalwork. Fire in 1851 gutted the area, and architect Walter rebuilt with cast iron. By 1890 need for room—bagged items stood in mid-floor— sparked a drive for the Library's own building, finished in 1897. Offices now occupy the former space. The Library today is probably the world's largest; its 54 million items echo Jefferson's remark that "there is no subject to which a Member of Congress may not have occasion to refer."*

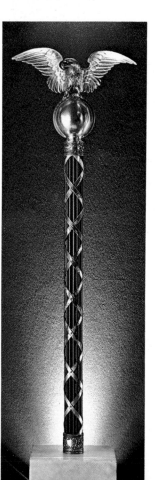

CARRYING THE MACE, *symbol of authority in the House, Sergeant at Arms rounds up Members for a quorum. This 1881 artist's conception appeared in* Leslie's *weekly. Actually, the mace rests on a stand beside the rostrum except in rare cases when displayed before an unruly Member to restore order. Its position at the rostrum tells whether the House is in "committee" or "session" —an aid for determining the number needed for a quorum.*

The first House mace was destroyed when the British burned the Capitol. A painted wood facsimile substituted until 1841, when a silver-and-ebony copy of the original was made (left). Its eagle and globe surmount rods representing the first 13 states. Length is 46 inches.

OATH-TAKING CEREMONY *of Vice President Theodore Roosevelt, March 4, 1901, finds President-elect William McKinley (center) and robed Chief Justice Melville Fuller among spectators. Until 1937 Vice Presidents were sworn in the Senate Chamber; since then, outdoors.*

leaky ship, heavy gales, and other hazards on an eight months' journey to the United States. By October, 1862, the bronze form was cast at Clark Mills' foundry in Maryland and Washingtonians had an opportunity to inspect the 19½-foot figure temporarily displayed on the Capitol grounds.

Finally, at the appointed hour of 12 noon, December 2, 1863, the giant head of Freedom—last of the statue's five sections—was raised and bolted into place.

The United States flag, bearing 35 stars for all the states, Northern and Southern, fluttered overhead. Spectators cheered. Capitol Hill's field battery boomed a 35-gun salute, one for each state. In turn a dozen Union forts rimming Washington roared back a pledge of 35-gun responses.

The Capitol was crowned, but not yet complete. The east portico of the new Senate wing had been finished in the fall of 1864, but several more years passed before its north and west entrances were in place. By 1867 all the porticoes of the Representatives' wing also had been built, but it was 1916 before the sculptured east pediment for the House was at last unveiled.

Today, the Capitol rejoices in a major addition—a 32½-foot eastward extension of the central area. This substantial enlargement in 1955 won the support of the late Sam Rayburn, Member of the House for 48 years and its Speaker for 17, who steered bills containing the proposal past Congressional hurdles.

President Eisenhower laid the extension's

cornerstone on July 4, 1959. A Masonic ceremony followed. Work went forward under the direction of Capitol Architect J. George Stewart, and the new front was ready just in time for President John F. Kennedy's inauguration on January 20, 1961.

Nearly a century earlier Walter had called such construction "an architectural necessity" to balance the added wings and Dome. Succeeding Capitol architects recommended the expansion against an outcry that no change should be made in America's treasured historic monument. The protests rose sharply when Congress in 1956 and again in 1958 took action in favor of the controversial construction. Yet many of its severest critics now agree that the new East Front has added beauty and much-needed working space.

Pushing the building's midsection forward eliminated the impression that the huge Dome overhung the central portico. The builders preserved, as interior supports, the walls that stood when General Lafayette visited the Rotunda. At the same time they replaced the old sandstone front with one of durable marble, every detail of hand-carved decoration faithfully copied from the crumbling originals.

Sandblasters laboriously took 32 layers of paint from the ironwork of the Dome. The replacement coats—requiring 1,750 gallons—were toned to match the marble of the wings, cleaned to pristine whiteness for the first time since 1862.

INSIDE, the Capitol gained two and a half acres of space spread over five floors. Brought into being were 102 rooms, including individual offices, committee and reception rooms, dining rooms, kitchens, and entrance foyers. There are additional elevators and—by no means the least of the innovations—private corridors linking north and south wings. At long last, Members of Congress can walk between Senate and House Chambers without having to elbow their way through sightseeing crowds.

But will the Capitol ever be finished? Studies have already been made for a four-level, 1,900-car garage, under the Capitol Plaza. The Architect of the Capitol has proposed an extension of the West Front,

and substitution of marble for the badly deteriorated sandstone of Bulfinch's construction. One light-hearted suggestion even called for an outdoor restaurant, with umbrella-shaded tables, as a pleasant way to use the stone terrace facing the Washington Monument and the White House.

The need for more space in which to conduct the increasing activities of Congress already has resulted in five huge office buildings nearby, two for the Senate and

three for the House. The third House Office Building was completed in 1965.

Surprisingly, Congress provided no working space outside the Capitol until 1908, when the first House Office Building opened. Before that, Members often rented their own in downtown Washington.

With each new office building have also come enlarged Capitol grounds, now totaling 131 acres. This stately park holds an unusually fine collection of American and

HUSHED JOINT SESSION *hears President Woodrow Wilson in 1917 ask Congress for a declaration of war to make the world "safe for democracy." Four years earlier he had shattered precedent by becoming the first Chief Executive to address Congress in person since John Adams in 1800. Beneath the flag, Vice President Thomas Marshall and Speaker Champ Clark (in light suit) preside.*

59

HUGO H. HARPER

PRESIDENT COOLIDGE *bestows the Medal of Honor on Charles A. Lindbergh for his historic flight across the Atlantic. Popularly called the "Congressional" medal, this highest of the Nation's decorations is awarded by the President in the name of Congress for "gallantry and intrepidity at the risk of life." Others in the 1928 picture at the White House are Speaker Nicholas Longworth, Vice President Charles G. Dawes, and Secretary of War Dwight Davis.*

LAUREL WREATH *and goddess Minerva embellish the Army's Medal of Honor. Reverse here bears Lindbergh citation. Navy version differs slightly in design.*

foreign trees, as well as many shrubs and flowers. In 1965, azaleas, tulips, and annuals were planted, and remodeling of terraces is planned.

Much of the Capitol's landscaping was done in the mid-1870's by Frederick Law Olmsted, who also designed New York's Central Park.

In those days, certain areas at the Capitol served for croquet games, and others for egg rolling by children at Easter. But perhaps the sharpest reminder of a vanished era appears in a routine report of 1877. Plants and bushes, it said, had been damaged by stray neighborhood cows.

Since such rustic incidents the Capitol has both reflected and affected the changes that have swept the country and the world. It has seen Congress grow to 100 Senators and 435 Representatives, plus a Resident Commissioner from Puerto Rico. So steadily did population expansion boost House membership that Congress, worried over the possibility of an unwieldy number, in 1911 limited the total to the present 435.

The U. S. Congress belies the saying that those who make a nation's songs mold its character. In

BLINDFOLDED *with a cloth from a chair in Independence Hall, Secretary of War Henry L. Stimson begins the 1940 draft—first ever enacted by Congress in peacetime. President Roosevelt read the number Stimson drew, 158. The same bowl did duty in the 1917 draft.*

J. GEORGE STEWART, *appointed Architect of the Capitol in 1954 by President Eisenhower, carried out the building's first major face change in nearly a century. But this East Front extension has been only one of the achievements in his tenure as eighth in the office. Others include the huge Rayburn House Office Building, the new Senate Office Building, and purchase of land about the Capitol for park use and expansion.*

Born in 1890, Stewart graduated from the University of Delaware. He had a varied career as builder, surveyor, engineering consultant, Member of Congress, and Clerk of the District of Columbia Committee of the Senate before taking his present post. Early predecessors had varied titles; first to be officially called Architect of the Capitol was Charles Bulfinch. Besides construction, the office's duties today take in repair and maintenance—even statue dusting.

GRANITE CORNERSTONE, *third to be laid by a President at the Capitol, goes into place July 4, 1959. President Eisenhower used the same trowel and gavel Washington and Fillmore had employed earlier.*

OFFICE OF THE ARCHITECT OF THE CAPITOL; FRED MAROON (RIGHT)

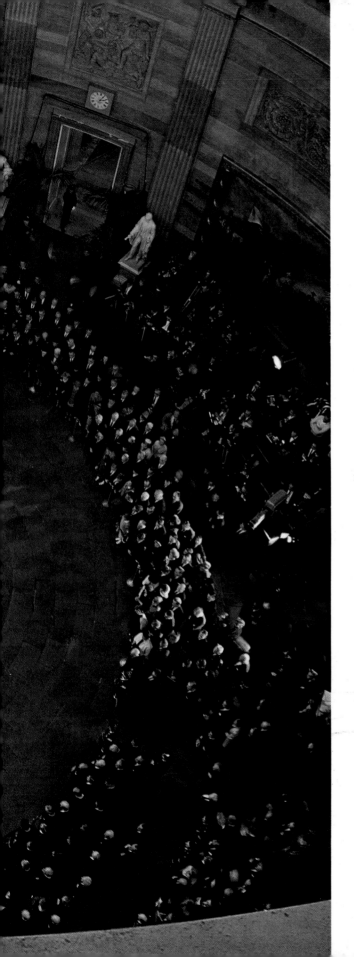

laws passed here, a knowledgeable student can trace the course of modern America's economic, political, and social development.

Between the lines of Reconstruction legislation, he can feel the passions and furies of bitter adjustments. Thumbing through successive homestead acts, he can almost hear the "whoop and holler" with which each wave of pioneers took over the Government's freely offered acres for farmlands, timber, and cattle-raising.

The rise of big industry and high finance—based on seemingly endless raw materials and subject to boom-and-bust speculation— brought regulation in such fields as interstate commerce, pure foods and drugs, trusts and monopolies, and conservation of natural resources.

President McKinley's war message to Congress in 1898 not only

FLAG-DRAPED, *the casket of John F. Kennedy rests in the Rotunda as dignitaries lead a Nation's mourning for its murdered President. Beginning with Lincoln, 19 honored dead have lain in state under the Capitol Dome.*

Congressmen, Government officials, and other noted persons encircle the catafalque in the November 24, 1963, memorial services. Later the public filed by in lines four people abreast. The queues stretched for 40 blocks.

Youngest elected President, Kennedy was eighth to die in office. Like him, McKinley, Garfield, and Lincoln fell before an assassin's gun; Harrison, Taylor, Harding, and Franklin Roosevelt succumbed to illness.

STATESMEN, AUTHORS—*many persons have addressed Congress. For Presidents and on rare occasions, the houses sit in Joint Session; for others, in Joint Meeting. Among guests: Winston Churchill, Carl Sandburg, John Glenn.*

SENATE AND HOUSE *meet in Joint Session to hear President Johnson's 1964 State of the Union Message. Mr. Johnson stands alone on the intermediary dais in the House Chamber. Supreme Court Justices, Cabinet Members, and the Joint Chiefs of Staff sit in temporary seats around the rostrum. Senators fill forward rows, Representatives the rear ones. Reporters pack gallery desks behind the clock. Space remaining goes to special guests.*

launched the short Spanish-American War, it marked the renewal of United States participation in world politics on a significant scale. Within 50 years, after many debates, membership in regional pacts and the United Nations linked this country with many others throughout the world.

Twentieth-century Americans can look back on dozens of laws that have drastically transformed the Nation and their personal lives. To mention a few of poignant memory: The income tax amendment of 1913, woman suffrage in 1920, prohibition and its repeal, and a whole body of New Deal legislation, such as the far-reaching Social Security Act of 1935.

All this, and more, has been built into the United States Capitol, and is part of what a visitor may see and sense as he walks through the home of Congress.

Exploring Today's Capitol

STAND ON the Capitol plaza, facing the monumental east steps. There you occupy a front-line spot from which Americans have witnessed Presidential inaugurals since Andrew Jackson brought the ceremony out to cheering followers in 1829.

Architect Bulfinch's central portico had just been completed then. Spilling out from the plaza before it was a milling crowd of bankers, workmen, and housewives, town merchants and visiting frontiersmen, some of whom had walked far to see the triumph of the "People's President." Between the portico's towering columns and on its stone steps stood Washington's great and their ladies. "Scarlet, purple, blue, yellow, white draperies and waving plumes of every kind and colour . . . had a fine effect," wrote a social commentator of the times.

On a platform built above those steps, Lincoln near the end of fratricidal war spoke the compassionate words, "With malice toward none, with charity for all. . . ." There Franklin D. Roosevelt told a Nation trying to lift itself from paralyzing depression, "the only thing we have to fear is fear itself." And John F. Kennedy said, "ask not what your country can do for you, ask what you can do for your country."

From Jackson to Lyndon Johnson, 25 Presidents have been inaugurated at the East Front. On the portico's pediment above them, three sculptured figures looked down. They represent America flanked by Justice and Hope.

The decoration was suggested by President John Quincy Adams during the Bulfinch construction. The President named a committee to help choose the design; his own proposal to use the three classical female figures was the one finally adopted. Adams favored Hope with an anchor as "a Scriptural image, indicating that this Hope relies upon a Supreme Disposer of events." He discarded a figure of Hercules as smacking "too much of the heathen mythology."

Look up and beyond the figured pediment. Towering there is the Dome, mute and immobile. But is it? Unseen, the iron structure moves at the whim of sun and wind.

Measurements reported nearly a century ago found that progressive sections of the double-walled 4,455-ton Dome bulged and receded as much as four inches from expansion and contraction on days of extreme temperature. A recording device hung from a wire reaching up into the Dome's top traced a wild pattern at the Rotunda floor as the iron cap swayed in the wind.

Walk through that pedimented portico dominated by the great Dome. Step past the statues of War and Peace; the Italian artist Luigi Persico, who carried out the pediment adornment, also designed them. And pause then before the massive bronze doors leading to the Capitol Rotunda.

Many connoisseurs feel that these 10-ton portals, the work of the American sculptor Randolph Rogers, rank with the world's best sculpture of the kind. In high relief on panels of gleaming bronze, figures portray events in the life of Columbus.

Rogers modeled his doors in Rome during the 1850's, and had them cast in the famous Royal Bavarian Foundry of Munich. They were first installed inside the Capitol at the entrance to the Old House Chamber, then in 1871 moved to this position so more people could enjoy their beauty.

Pass through the doors and into the Rotunda. You stand now at the heart of the Capitol and at the hub of streets leading north, south, east, and west from its grounds. Here is another case of built-in symbolism

WASHINGTON IN BRONZE *stands against the monumental background of the Dome's interior. Figures in the overhead painting—an allegorical glorification of the first President—were drawn as much as 15 feet high to seem life-size from the Rotunda floor 180 feet below. Perspective here hides part of the fresco behind a balcony around the eye of the Dome.*

going back to the decision of Washington and L'Enfant to place the Congress House at the mid-point of the city they envisioned. Later boundary changes, however, put the Federal District's geographical center some 20 blocks away.

The huge circular hall—nearly 100 feet across and more than 180 feet high—is the heart also of the Capitol's historic art displays. Beginning here and extending into Senate and House wings spreads a maze of rooms and corridors. Many are filled with sculpture and paintings collected by Congress over the years through purchase, gift, or commissions to artists.

O N ENCIRCLING WALLS of the Rotunda hang eight immense oil paintings. Four depict happenings from fledgling days of discovery and colonization. One of these, "The Baptism of Pocahontas" by John Chapman, attracts visitors seeking the Indian with six toes the artist painted into the picture. A direct descendant of Pocahontas, the acid-tongued John Randolph of Roanoke, two centuries later sat in the halls of Congress as Representative and Senator.

The other four are priceless links with the American struggle for independence. Painted while memories of the Revolution were still alive in the hearts and minds of leaders shown here, they represent the Declaration of Independence, the surrenders of General Burgoyne and Lord Cornwallis, and General Washington resigning his commission.

The artist, John Trumbull, served briefly in the war as an aide to Washington. He knew many of his subjects well, and had traveled far to obtain likenesses. He painted John Adams in London, when the future U. S. President was Minister to England. In Paris, amid rumblings of the French Revolution, he made a portrait of Jefferson, then Minister to the royal government.

"I have been in this capital of dissipation and nonsense near six weeks," Trumbull wrote his brother Jonathan in 1788, "for the purpose of getting the portraits of the French Officers who were at York Town, and have happily been ... successfull."

Such human stories, repeated by successive generations of Americans, are like fam-

BRONZE "COLUMBUS DOORS" *give entry to the Rotunda. Young admirers (right) view details depicting events in the discoverer's life. Doorway lunette portrays his landing; four figures on the frame symbolize continents.*

Randolph Rogers modeled the doors in the 1850's. One of its panels (top) pictures Columbus at La Rábida friary, where he had come dejected, but left buoyed with new hope of seeing Queen Isabella. Panel below shows his return in chains after his third voyage. Vandals stole links that once joined the figure's wrists.

ily anecdotes told of favorite ancestors. They breathe spirit into the sculpture around the Rotunda's sweeping walls.

One, the tall, commanding figure of Washington, is a bronze copy of Jean Houdon's true-to-life statue displayed in the State Capitol at Richmond, Virginia.

On either side of Washington stand Jefferson and Hamilton, whose political bargain gave the Federal Capital its Potomac site.

Treasury Secretary Hamilton was seeking legislation at the time to have the national Government assume state debts incurred during the Revolution. Encountering Jefferson near the President's house when New York was the temporary seat of government, Hamilton persuaded the Virginian to use his influence with Southern legislators to win votes for debt assumption. In return, the Southerners were offered Northern support in locating the permanent Capital nearer their part of the country.

The agreement bore fruit, as we know, in the act of 1790 that established the Government's residence beside the Potomac. But it brought gibes at the time. One newspaper wrote that "Miss Assumption," beguiled

HEROIC FIGURES *display time-enhanced colors in this close-up of the Dome's "Apotheosis of Washington." To cover the 4,664 square feet of concave surface, Constantino Brumidi often lay on his back on a scaffold. He worked in fresco—pigment applied to newly troweled plaster; parts not completed before the plaster dries must be scraped off and redone. Chemical changes as the mortar sets add to beauty and permanence of color. Brumidi, then 60, did his masterpiece in 11 months, signing it in 1865.*

Forms in the inner circle represent the 13 original states and the Union; Washington sits between Liberty and laureled Victory. Outer groups—clockwise from sword-wielding Freedom— symbolize arts and sciences, marine, commerce, mechanics, and agriculture.

GODS AND MORTALS *mingle in the Dome's fresco. Sandaled Mercury offers a bag of gold to Robert Morris, "financier of the* *Revolution." Vulcan rests his foot on a cannon. Ceres rides a reaper as Young America, wearing liberty cap, stands near*

*Bearded Neptune and Aphrodite, holding the
Atlantic cable, rise from the sea. Wise
Minerva speaks to Benjamin Franklin, S. F. B.*

*Morse, and Robert Fulton. Armed Freedom
—Brumidi's young wife was the model—
triumphs over Tyranny and Kingly Power*

SCULPTURED SHARPNESS *in wall-flat fresco panoramas the Nation's history on the Rotunda frieze. Brumidi began it, but died while painting Penn's treaty with the Indians. Filippo Costaggini continued the work (right) from Brumidi sketches. Allyn Cox added a final section in 1953.*

by the promises of "Mr. Residence," had given birth to the child "Potowmacus."

Memories of the War of 1812 cling to the slim bronze of Gen. Andrew Jackson, seen here in the uniform and dashing cape he wore as the victor of the Battle of New Orleans. Considering today's fast-as-light communications, it is ironic to recall that the battle was fought before either side knew peace had already been signed.

As President in 1835, "Old Hickory" nearly lost his life near the spot where you now see his statue. He had attended funeral services for a Member of Congress in the House Chamber, and was about to leave the Rotunda when a man stepped out from the crowd and aimed a pistol point-blank. The gun misfired. He whipped out a second hidden by his cloak. It, too, misfired in this, the first attempt to assassinate a U. S. President. The assailant was found insane.

Another era, the most tragic in the Nation's history, comes to mind as you pass the stocky, down-to-earth form of Ulysses S. Grant, in his rumpled field uniform.

"I can't spare this man," Lincoln once replied to Grant's detractors. "He fights."

But, some may ask, who was Edward D. Baker, whose toga-draped statue has a place among America's most celebrated leaders?

An Oregon Senator, formerly of Illinois, "Ned" Baker was Lincoln's intimate friend, chosen for the honor of introducing the President for his first inaugural address.

As a Union commander, Baker was killed seven months later in the ill-fated foray at Ball's Bluff, on the Virginia side of the Potomac. Lincoln heard the news as it came clicking in over the telegraph wires at the War Department. He left soon after, a correspondent wrote, "with bowed head and tears rolling down his furrowed cheeks."

Today's visitors often stand quietly before a giant marble head and a life-size marble statue set together in the Rotunda. Both

(Continued on page 82)

CONSTANTINO BRUMIDI *fled from Rome in his late 40's to escape political persecution. He had been born there in 1805, studied at the Academy of Arts, and gained repute by restoring Vatican frescoes. Coming to the United States, he spent a quarter-century—for pay averaging $3,200 a year—working "to make beautiful the Capitol of the one country on earth in which there is liberty." He slipped from a scaffold in 1879 while painting the Rotunda frieze, but managed to grasp a precarious hold and hang 58 feet above the floor until help came. The shock, however, hurried his death a few months later. Mathew Brady photographed him with brush and palette in the 1860's.*

77

VISITORS SHRINK *to doll size when seen from the topmost balcony within the Dome. Once the public could climb twisting, narrow stairs to this lofty walkway. But so many persons collapsed and had to be carried down, and so much trash was tossed below, that the area was closed. Frescoed figures march in an endless band around the Rotunda's frieze. The railings just above guard the Dome's lower balcony. A camera hung from a rope across the chasm made this picture.*

TOP HATS AND BUSTLES *identify 1871 tourists. They saw, said a newspaper account, the world's "most wretched collection" of art. A protest leap, it added, would be "justifiable suicide."*

"DISCOVERY OF THE MISSISSIPPI" *hangs in the Rotunda with seven other historical paintings, each measuring about 14 by 20 feet. William H. Powell shows De Soto on horseback, with the river in the background.*

"EMBARKATION OF THE PILGRIMS," *by Robert W. Weir, had a falling beam strike it during Dome construction. In the group, setting sail from Holland, William Brewster holds a Bible, Miles Standish leans on a sword.*

"DECLARATION OF INDEPENDENCE" *by Revolutionary artist John Trumbull depicts the drafting committee—led by red-waistcoated Thomas Jefferson—presenting the document to John Hancock and the Continental Congress.*

"SURRENDER OF CORNWALLIS" *at Yorktown, by Trumbull. When the British general—professing indisposition—sent a subordinate, Washington (astride a brown charger) had Benjamin Lincoln accept the capitulation.*

are of Abraham Lincoln. The head was carved, long after Lincoln's death, by the noted sculptor Gutzon Borglum. Its powerful characterization came from profound analysis of the man, looking "beyond the queer hat, bad tailoring, and boots you could not now give away," as Borglum wrote.

"You will find written on his face literally all the complexity of his great nature," the sculptor said, ". . . half smile, half sadness; half anger, half forgiveness . . . a dual nature struggling with a dual problem, delivering a single result."

Behind Lincoln's full-length statue lies another story, seldom told, of talented Vinnie Ream. Vinnie, shy and 17, had begun to attract notice in wartime Washington for her artistic skill when she was fired with a dream of creating a likeness of the President. A friend and advisor, Representative James Rollins of Missouri, called on Lincoln, asking permission for his protégée to make sketches in the White House. The President, preoccupied by the war, paid scant attention until Rollins happened to mention that the girl was poor.

STATUARY HALL, *with traditional color restored, welcomes visitors. "Liberty" stands over south door; opposite it, "Car of History" (above). Muse Clio in the chariot records events; the clock once told time for the House.*

WHISPERS ECHO *in the hall. Mrs. Myrtle C. Murdock, Capitol guide and Brumidi authority, demonstrates; schoolboys group in the spot where John Quincy Adams was fatally stricken.*

"So she's young and poor, is she. Well, that's nothing agin' her," Lincoln said, slipping into a colloquialism. "You may tell her she can come."

In half-hour sessions at the White House during the last five months of the President's life, Vinnie sketched away. She watched while he met official callers and handled the heavy burdens of the day. Later, she worked it all into this marble form of a melancholy man with thoughtful, downward gaze.

A MOURNING NATION has paid final tribute to 19 of its sons in the Rotunda. Four murdered Presidents—Lincoln, Garfield, McKinley, and Kennedy—lay in state while silent crowds filed by.

When Kennedy's casket rested here, the lines stretched 40 blocks outside the Capitol. Inside, stone and painted figures of the past looked down on ceremonies for the man who had had a special sense of history. And saw, too, a timeless tragedy as his widow knelt beside the flag-draped casket with her now fatherless little girl, Caroline.

In post-Civil War years, two passionate opponents of slavery, Representative Thaddeus Stevens and Senator Charles Sumner, were accorded the honor. So were Henry Wilson, Grant's Vice President, and Union general and Illinois Senator John A. Logan, who initiated the Memorial Day observance.

There was L'Enfant, whose disinterred remains were brought here in 1909 in belated recognition of his genius. And after L'Enfant came Adm. George Dewey of Manila fame; the Unknown Soldier of World War I; President Warren G. Harding; and Chief Justice and former President William Howard Taft, the only man to hold both offices.

Before sorrowing witnesses lay also the body of Gen. John J. Pershing, commander of the American Expeditionary Forces in World War I, and those of the Unknowns of World War II and Korea. In 1953, the nation's highest final honor went to Senator Robert A. Taft, as it had to his father 23 years before. And in 1964, General of the Army Douglas MacArthur and former President Herbert Hoover joined the company of illustrious dead who had lain in state on the Capitol's black catafalque.

But sadness has no part in the Rotunda's everyday activities. Mostly this room is a place of holiday crowds, honeymoon couples, and children fascinated by a thousand and one strange new sights.

"It's like St. Peter's in Rome," tourists sometimes say, as they look up into the soaring Dome, cut by windows through which light filters softly.

Across the Dome's eye, 180 feet above the floor, spreads a gigantic allegorical painting by the Italian

MARBLE FIGURES *stare from bulky pedestals in Statuary Hall. The House Chamber until 1857, it became a showcase for statues of noted individuals after a period of abandonment to "dust, tobacco, and apple pomace." Each state may place likenesses of two of its sons or daughters in this national hall of fame. Men shown here are Georgia's Alexander H. Stephens, Utah's Brigham Young, Vermont's Ethan Allen, Idaho's George L. Shoup, and South Carolina's John C. Calhoun.*

artist Constantino Brumidi. The painting depicts the "Apotheosis," or glorification, of George Washington. Surrounding Washington in sweeping circles are delicately colored figures—some 15 feet tall. They include gods and goddesses pictured as protectors of American ideals and progress.

Like most of Brumidi's work through the Capitol, the Dome decoration was done in true fresco. In this exacting technique, used by Michelangelo in the Sistine Chapel, the artist applies pigments to fresh plaster. Brumidi, often lying on his back high on a scaffold, had to paint fast, lest the plaster dry and force him to rework a whole section.

To the dedicated artist, however, nothing was too much trouble for his adopted coun-try. Born in Rome of Greek descent, Brumidi had fled his homeland in 1852 and found political refuge in the United States. He showed his gratitude by laboring from 1855 to 1880 to cover the Capitol's interior with vivid, patriotic designs.

"C. Brumidi, artist. Citizen of the U. S.," he signed his huge mural on the surrender at Yorktown, now in the House Restaurant.

"My one ambition," he wrote after success brought offers of other commissions, "... is that I may live long enough to make beautiful the Capitol of the one country on earth in which there is liberty."

Brumidi was 60 when he finished the Dome canopy, and 72 when he set up his scaffold below to begin his long-planned

frieze showing scenes from American history. He completed six panels, a third of the expanse 300 feet around and eight feet high. Then one day, while painting the seventh, Penn's treaty with the Indians, he suddenly lost his balance. Desperately he grabbed the platform and clung—58 feet from the floor—until rescuers came.

But Brumidi's working days were nearly over. He died a few months later, and Congress commissioned his pupil, Filippo Costaggini, to execute the remaining panels. Costaggini spent eight years translating to full scale the eight small sketches left by Brumidi. A 30-foot gap remained in 1888 on completion of the last one. It was not until 1953 that the blank was finally filled in, by a third fresco artist, Allyn Cox of New York.

In this remarkable painted frieze that looks like sculpture, you can pick out the three most recent panels by their subjects: the Civil War, the Spanish-American War, and the birth of aviation, illustrated by the Wright brothers' flight of 1903.

In nearby Statuary Hall, converted from the room in which the House met between 1807 and 1857, visitors gaze curiously at a unique collection of bronze and marble statues. Presented by 48 states in memory of distinguished citizens of the past, these figures honor pioneers, missionaries, teachers, soldiers, physicians, inventors, statesmen, and others who made major contributions to their states and their country.

Here, in commanding pose, stands Ethan Allen, Vermont's Revolutionary hero who, tradition has it, demanded the surrender of Ticonderoga "in the name of the Great Jehovah and the Continental Congress." Over there sits a thoughtful young man

CONGRESSIONAL LADIES' *Retiring Room was once the office of the Speaker of the House. To it colleagues carried John Quincy Adams when he was stricken as he waited to vote in the House Chamber; the couch (below) on which he died still graces the room. Former Congresswoman Marguerite Stitt Church (center) chats with Representatives Charlotte T. Reid (left), Frances P. Bolton, Edna F. Kelly, and Patsy T. Mink.*

FREDERICK MUHLENBERG— *first to be elected Speaker, 1789.*

HENRY CLAY—*molded the Speakership to its powerful role.*

SAM RAYBURN—*served longest, 17 years. The Speaker is second in succession to the Presidency.*

PORTRAITS *line the Speaker's Lobby. Awaiting a House session (from left): Reps. Omar Burleson, Samuel L. Devine, Parliamentarian Lewis Deschler, Rep. E. Ross Adair, Dr. Martin Sweig, Capt. L. H. Ballard, Sergeant at Arms Z. W. Johnson, Jr., Rep. H. R. Gross, J. L. Monahan, Reps. Melvin Price, J. Edward Roush.*

REPRESENTATIVES SIT *for the first official photograph of the House in session, voting on a tax reduction bill February 25, 1964. Gray marble behind the rostrum and in pilasters accents the room's walnut paneling. State seals border the ceiling; noted lawgivers from Hammurabi to Jefferson appear above gallery doors. John Vanderlyn's portrait of Washington and Ary Scheffer's Lafayette hang on the rostrum wall. In the large inset, officials of the House staff occupy seats below Speaker John W. McCormack; small insets show leaders of the Majority (top) and Minority (left).*

CLERK OF THE HOUSE *W. Pat Jennings (center) must sign each bill passed. With him are Reps. Charles A. Halleck (left) and Barratt O'Hara.*

HOUSE READING ROOM *just off the Speaker's Lobby files hometown papers. Seated (from left): Dr. Edward G. Latch, House Chaplain; Reps. Leslie C. Arends, Hale Boggs, Melvin R. Laird. Standing: Charles E. Goodell, John J. Rhodes, Robert E. Jones, Jr., Kenneth J. Gray, and Omar Burleson.*

WALNUT PANELING *enriches the House Reception Room. Here Members may meet guests. At foreground table: Representative Wright Patman, Mrs. Winston L. Prouty, Mrs. John C. Kunkel, Representative Florence P. Dwyer.*

NATIONAL GEOGRAPHIC PHOTOGRAPHERS ROBERT S. OAKES (LEFT) AND JAMES P. BLAIR (ABOVE)

examining a model of a steamboat—Robert Fulton of Pennsylvania.

Looking at the quill pen held by Maryland's Charles Carroll, you recall a defiant patriot; he added "of Carrollton" to his signature on the Declaration of Independence to make distinguishing him easy.

And the name "John Gorrie M.D." engraved on the statue contributed by Florida identifies the ingenious doctor who experimented with devices to cool the rooms of his fevered patients and who in 1851 patented the first ice-making machine.

A number of the men now standing in marble and bronze on pedestals lining the walls of Statuary Hall were Members of Congress who knew this room well during its half century as the House Chamber. Clay, Calhoun, and Webster sat as Representatives here in their early careers. Clay served as Speaker, ruling from the throne-

BRONZE AND MARBLE *alternate in statues of the Hall of Columns—often called "Tobacco Hall" because of its brown walls and tobacco-leaf capitals. State notables flank the posts. Shown here: Florida's Confederate Gen. Edmund Kirby-Smith, Kansas' pioneer Governor George W. Glick, Mississippi's "Great Commoner" James Z. George, West Virginia's Senator John E. Kenna, New Jersey's "perfect soldier" Gen. Philip Kearny, Massachusetts' John Winthrop.*

REPEATING BEAMS *and pillars of the Hall of Columns find a model in Athens' Temple of the Winds. Statues are California's Thomas S. King (bronze), Indiana's Oliver P. Morton.*

like Speaker's chair on a platform canopied in crimson and green draperies.

No statue commemorates the 17 years of courageous and conscientious service rendered by another great statesman, John Quincy Adams. But Statuary Hall honors Adams with a small bronze plate marking the spot where he was felled by a stroke on February 21, 1848. He died in the Speaker's Office just off the Chamber.

By coincidence, the Adams plate also marks the best place to demonstrate the room's strange acoustics that so annoyed early Members. Standing where Adams stood, you can hear a whisper spoken across the room, though it is inaudible close by.

TRANSFORMATION of the Old House Chamber into a national gallery of fame began a hundred years ago, after the abandoned legislative hall had become, in the words of an investigating committee, "worse than uselessly occupied as a place of storage and traffic. . . ."

It was "draped in cobwebs and carpeted with dust," said Representative Justin S. Morrill of Vermont in debate on the resolution to turn it into an exhibit hall.

"I look to see where Calhoun sat . . . and where Clay sat and I find a woman selling oranges and root beer," remarked a colleague in supporting the measure.

As passed in July, 1864, the bill cleared out the hucksters who had invaded the room, and authorized the President to invite each state to contribute two statues representing outstanding deceased citizens.

First to arrive—from Rhode Island in 1870—was a statue of Nathanael Greene, fighting Quartermaster General in the Revolution, who poured out his own fortune to supply needy soldiers. Gradually others followed, until their combined weight in the early 1930's raised fears that the whole assemblage might crash through the floor. Since then Statuary Hall has been limited to one statue per state. The others have been placed in the Hall of Columns on the House side or elsewhere around the building.

So far, the Capitol's roster of state notables includes 84 favorite sons and four favorite daughters. First woman so honored was Frances E. Willard of Illinois, temperance

leader and college president. "She possessed all the qualities of organization which have made such men as Marshall Field, Morgan, and Carnegie multi-millionaires," said Illinois Senator Albert J. Hopkins when the statue was received in 1905.

The other three memorials on the distaff side have all been presented since 1959. Wyoming chose Esther Hobart Morris, who made history as the world's first woman justice of the peace, and who helped persuade Wyoming to become the first to adopt woman suffrage. Minnesota immortalized Maria Sanford, educator and civic leader—called the "best loved woman" in her state. Colorado sent a likeness of Dr.

Florence Rena Sabin, the first woman member of the National Academy of Sciences. You see her portrayed as she used to sit on her laboratory stool, microscope at her side.

Proving that Congress can take a joke, the Capitol also exhibits a statue of Oklahoma's famous cowboy humorist, Will Rogers, who never lost a chance to josh the members of what he called the Washington "joke factory." When the politicians "get in that immense Hall," said Will, "they begin to get Serious, and it's then that they do such Amusing things."

Just outside Statuary Hall, you find the familiar, easygoing figure, cast in bronze,

DELEGATES SIGN *the Constitution after its final drafting, September 17, 1787. The painting, acquired by Congress in 1940, hangs at the east stairway of the House wing. Artist Howard Chandler Christy worked in a Navy sail loft on the 20-by-30-foot canvas. It shows George Washington, presiding, with the Constitution's framers in Independence Hall. Alexander Hamilton talks to Benjamin Franklin (with cane). James Madison, the document's chief architect, sits at the table to Franklin's left.*

97

of the man whose homespun quips on politics brought him an opportunity to address an audience of Members of Congress and other Washington notables. At the hilarious 1933 gathering, Rogers solemnly informed Vice President John Nance Garner that he could "stay awake tonight. . . . This is one speech you haven't heard a dozen times."

Nor is Will Rogers the only cowboy to be corralled among the frock-coated statesmen and uniformed generals. Not far away stands a seven-foot statue of Montana's roving cowboy-artist Charles Marion Russell, who recorded a dying era of men and beasts in the Old West.

"You never saw one of his paintings," Rogers wrote of his friend's work, "that you couldn't tell just what the Indian, the Horse, and Buffalo were thinking about."

More statues are added from time to time to the Nation's hall of fame with presentation and acceptance speeches in the Rotunda; a Western parade, including stagecoach, brass band, and cowboy and Indian admirers of the artist, escorted Russell's figure to the Capitol in 1959. Three states—New Mexico, Alaska, and Hawaii—have yet to contribute their first statue. Seven have still to send a second.

Besides its state exhibits, the Capitol also has collected over 400 other works of art in various forms, from portraits and panoramic paintings to statues and busts—including heads of five Presidents, 35 Vice Presidents, ten Chief Justices, and two Indian chiefs.

At every turn you see faces—severe or benign, young or old. They recall a saying

PAIRED COLUMNS *circle the aisles in the crypt below the Rotunda. Capitol planners had envisioned a memorial here over Washington's tomb, to be seen through an opening in the Rotunda floor. The President's heirs, however, declined to allow transfer of his remains from Mount Vernon. A marble block, waggishly called "Ladies in a Bathtub" and honoring three pioneer suffragettes, now stands amid the arches. White marble inlay marks the Capitol's hub.*

IRON GATES *bar the archway into the tomb intended for Washington under the crypt. Now it contains the velveted bier on which Lincoln's coffin rested while in the Rotunda. The same catafalque has been used for all others who have lain in state there since.*

NATIONAL GEOGRAPHIC PHOTOGRAPHER JAMES P. BLAIR

by Ralph Waldo Emerson: "... there is properly no history, only biography."

Twenty of the busts in the Vice President collection look out from niches around the walls of the Senate gallery—a reminder that the chief official duty of this office is to preside as President of the Senate.

John Adams, in ruffled stock, holds a spot here as Washington's Vice President. Adams was far from pleased by his election. He wrote his wife that his country had arranged for him "the most insignificant office that ever the invention of man contrived."

"I have now ... 'taken the veil,'" Theodore Roosevelt wrote a friend in 1901, after his election to the post.

Chester A. Arthur, among the 20 depicted in the Senate gallery, served as Vice President for only six months in 1881 before Garfield's assassination brought him the Presidency. Political enemies nicknamed him "His Accidency."

Yet despite such witticisms, only one Vice President has ever resigned. John C. Calhoun gave up the office in 1832 to return to the Senate as South Carolina's great spokesman on sectional issues.

In the Capitol's art array, tourists can find enough personalities to play a lively guessing game of who-was-who-and-why in the American past.

Presidential likenesses scattered about the building are the easiest to identify. Some are famous works, like Thomas Sully's paintings of Jefferson and Jackson, and por-

(Continued on page 106)

HOUSE

1. House Majority Conference Room
2. House Minority Conference Room
3. Congressional Ladies' Retiring Room
4. Office of the Speaker
5. House Reception Room
6. Committee on Ways and Means
7. Grand Staircase-East*
8. Formal Office of the Speaker
9. Parliamentarian
10. Members' Reading Rooms
11. Speaker's Lobby
12. House Chamber
13. Library
14. Cloakrooms
15. Committee on Appropriations
16. Grand Staircase-West*
17. House Minority Whip
18. Statuary Hall*
19. House Document Room
20. House Subcommittee on Foreign Affairs
21. Representative's Private Office
22. House Minority Leader's Office
23. Representative's Private Office
24. Prayer Room for House and Senate

*Open to the public

Old Sandstone Wall

ROT

EAST

SENATE

25-30. Senators' Private Offices
31. Senate Disbursing Office
32. Senate Minority Leader's Office
33. Secretary
34. Grand Staircase-West*
35. Chief Clerk
36. Bill Clerk and Journal Clerk
37. Official Reporters of Debates
38. President's Room*
39. The Marble Room
40. Senators' Private Lobby
41. Senate Chamber
42. Cloakrooms
43. Formal Office of the Vice President
44. Senate Reception Room*
45. Office of the Vice President
46. Senate Majority Leader's Office
47. Grand Staircase-East*
48. Senate Conference Room*
49. Executive Clerk
50. Old Senate Chamber
51. Senate Minority Whip
52. Small Senate Rotunda*
53-58. Senators' Private Offices

*Open to the public

UNDA

Old Sandstone Wall

FRONT

Rick Loomis

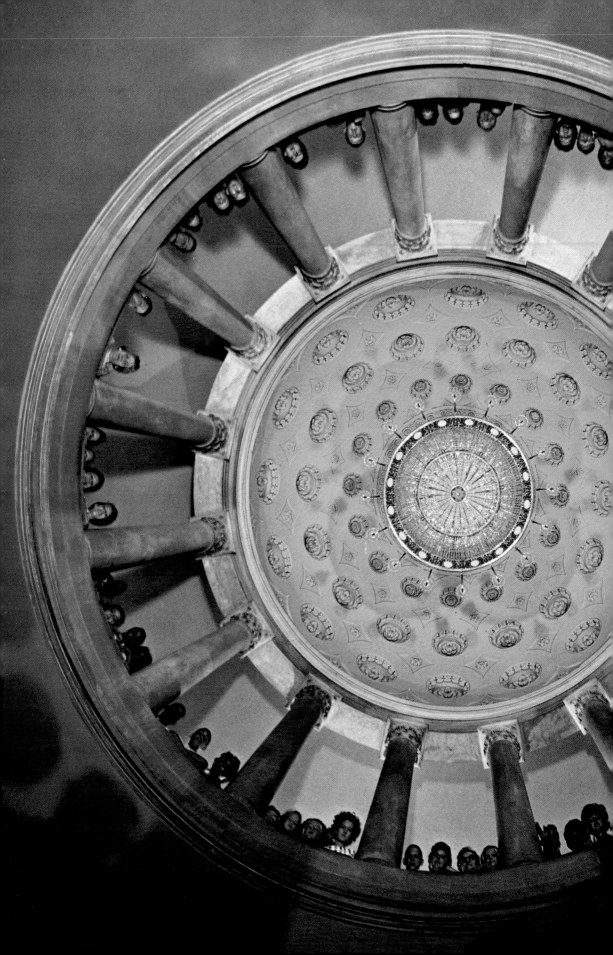

PEERING HEADS *create a living frieze around a balustrade in the Senate Rotunda. Architect Latrobe built this vestibule as a light well replacing stairs burned in the Capitol's 1814 fire. He gave capitals atop the 16 columns a motif of tobacco flowers and leaves—tribute to the plant's importance in the young Nation's economy.*

NATHANAEL GREENE, *Revolutionary hero, stands in stone in the Capitol— the first statue to be placed after states were invited thus to honor native sons.*

JOHN MARSHALL, *from 1801 to 1835 Chief Justice of the United States, helped mold the Supreme Court and the Nation with far-reaching opinions.*

WILLIAM HOWARD TAFT *found being Chief Justice "nearer to my heart" than being President. He served from 1921 to 1930.*

GILDED EAGLE *from Daniel Webster's day looks down on the marble-columned hall where the Senate and the Supreme Court once sat. The Justices occupied the chamber in 1860 after the Senate moved into its present wing. They remained until the Supreme Court Building was completed in 1935. Joint Committee on Atomic Energy returns to the chamber it used for public hearings before the East Front extension. Officials of the Atomic Energy Commission give reports: (standing, left) Commissioner James T. Ramey, (seated, from left) Commissioner John G. Palfrey, Chairman Glenn T. Seaborg, General Manager Robert E. Hollingsworth. The Committee (seated, from left) includes: Senators Carl T. Curtis, Henry M. Jackson, Wallace F. Bennett, Clinton P. Anderson, Bourke B. Hickenlooper, Richard B. Russell, John O. Pastore (Chairman), Representatives Chet Holifield (Vice Chairman), Wayne N. Aspinall, Craig Hosmer, William H. Bates, Thomas G. Morris, John B. Anderson, William M. McCulloch, John Young. Aides are (standing, from left) J. Bruce Burris, George F. Murphy, Jr., John T. Conway, Edward J. Bauser, (seated) Edith Jack. In the sketch at right, published in 1887, spectators listen as a lawyer addresses the Supreme Court. Busts of past Chief Justices line the walls.*

GILDED SPLENDOR *and bright frescoes decorate the Senate Reception Room; paintings of Taft, Calhoun, Webster, Clay, and La Follette were chosen in 1957 to fill panels Brumidi left vacant. Senators use this room to greet guests. From left: Edward M. Kennedy, Edward W. Brooke, Jacob K. Javits, B. Everett Jordan. In an 1873 engraving (below), carpeting hides the intricate tiles.*

traits of George Washington by Charles Willson Peale and Gilbert Stuart.

Others record historic events—such as a huge painting over the Senate's west stairway that shows Lincoln meeting with his Cabinet to read the Emancipation Proclamation. The artist, Francis Bicknell Carpenter, did the painting in the White House; Lincoln himself authenticated details.

But who were the Indian chiefs? They represent tribal leaders who visited Washington during the 1850's—a period when chieftains often came to the Capitol to sign treaties or seek redress for grievances.

Two of the busts are of Be-sheck-kee— "the Buffalo." A Chippewa, he posed for an Italian sculptor, Francis Vincenti, then employed at the Capitol. Vincenti produced the marble bust now shown in the Senate wing. Another Capitol artist made the bronze copy displayed on the House side.

It took sharp detective work some 50 years ago to identify the then mysterious third bust, another marble by Vincenti.

The help of the Government's Bureau of Indian Affairs was enlisted. Photographs went out to field agents around the country. One agent suggested—on the basis of a telltale ear scar the sculptor had faithfully reproduced—that the bust was of another Chippewa chief, Aysh-ke-bah-ke-ko-zhay, widely known as "Flat Mouth." Careful checking confirmed the identification.

Even more arresting than the Indian exhibits is an eight-ton block of marble down in the crypt, surmounted by heads of three

HISTORIC PHOTOGRAPH—*first official portrait ever made of the Senate in session—captures the vote ratifying the atomic test ban treaty, September 24, 1963. Unanimous consent was received to record the event for the United States Capitol Historical Society. Senators sit by seniority from front to rear, though some choose not to move forward when vacancies occur.*

BLOTTING SAND, *a heritage of days when the tradition-rich Senate had an official penmaker to cut goose-quill points, still is kept on each desk. The shakers now are used as paperweights.*

LACQUERED SNUFFBOXES, *kept filled with fresh snuff though no longer used, sit on ledges near the Senate rostrum. Senator Clay made trips to the boxes a signal to his followers.*

stern-looking Victorian ladies. Standing amid the massive columns and groined arches that support the Rotunda floor above, this monument honors a trio of pioneer suffragettes, Lucretia Mott, Elizabeth Cady Stanton, and Susan B. Anthony.

Modern sightseers smile at the group's nickname, the "Ladies in a Bathtub." But there was nothing comic about the gratitude of the American women in whose name a long list of women's organizations presented the memorial to the Capitol in 1921. In what was perhaps the gayest celebration the Rotunda ever knew, hundreds of women formed a procession after the dedication, circling the room and waving banners in the happy knowledge that they had recently won their long battle for woman suffrage.

At the end of vaulted corridors below the suffragettes, visitors may see the "tomb"—the spot where Congress once hoped to enshrine George Washington's body. Immediately after his death in 1799, Congress passed a joint resolution authorizing the erection of a monument to the first President at the heart of the future Capitol. His remains were to be transferred from Mount Vernon and placed in a space beneath the memorial.

The project was discussed, committees met, and correspondence was carried on with members of the Washington family.

During construction of the central section of the Capitol, a wide circular opening was left in the Rotunda floor to admit light and permit visitors to look down on Washington's memorial, as they do in Paris on the Tomb of Napoleon.

"The idea was poetical, grand, and captivating," commented John Trumbull. But he found that the damp air rising from the crypt was ruining his paintings of the Revolution, hung in the Rotunda in 1824. At Trumbull's urging, Capitol masons closed

SENATE LOBBY *just off the Chamber offers desks for writing and seats for private talks. In such rooms of public buildings in the past, individuals with pet projects buttonholed legislators, hence the term "lobbying." Rules today prohibit the public from going onto the floors of Senate or House during sessions. Here Senators Milton R. Young, Bourke B. Hickenlooper, Ralph W. Yarborough, and Spessard L. Holland confer.*

the floor opening in 1828. Four years later Washington's heirs decided against removing the General's remains from Mount Vernon. Congress at the same time voted to commission Horatio Greenough to make a statue of the Father of His Country.

Greenough draped his marble Washington in classic Greek style. The sight shocked the public when the statue was displayed in the center of the Rotunda in the early 1840's. As Capitol Architect Bulfinch had predicted, people wanted "to see the great man as their imagination has painted him." He feared the statue would "give the idea of entering or leaving a bath."

The heroic 20-ton figure was moved out to the grounds, then in 1908 transferred to the Smithsonian Institution.

Washington's tomb site, however, is not vacant. There you see a black-draped bier, protected from souvenir hunters by an iron gate. On this somber catafalque, first built for Lincoln, have rested the bodies of all the men who have lain in state in the Rotunda above since 1865.

Come up from the building's gloomy depths to the ground floor of the Senate wing. Here you walk on color, surrounded by more color—decorative art that covers wall and ceiling surfaces of corridors and committee rooms.

Underfoot, in blue, cream, and red, stretch glazed tiles made in the mid-1850's by the skilled craftsmen of England's Minton works. Though millions have trod these tiles, even worn them down in spots, the colors remain amazingly vivid.

On the walls, Brumidi painted in both oil and fresco. Laboring for years, he created incredibly varied designs of birds, animals,

MARBLE ROOM *adjoining the Senate Lobby displays Tennessee marble on its walls and Italian marble in columns and ceiling. The room—by official rule designated a part of the Senate floor—multiplies its elegance in reflections between mirrors on opposing walls. Here legislators relax or read newspapers from home; these Senators are (from left) Margaret Chase Smith, Robert C. Byrd, Henry M. Jackson, and Thomas H. Kuchel.*

Capitol visitors once dressed in high fashion, as this 1873 engraving (right) shows. Now sports shirts and shorts are seen— garb periodically criticized in Congressional comments and newspaper editorials.

BESPECTACLED FRANKLIN, *representing
"History," and Columbus, symbolizing
"Discovery," occupy panels in the Presi-
dent's Room. Painted frames of these
Brumidi frescoes seem three-dimensional.*

GOLD-FINISHED CHANDELIER *and Brumidi frescoes adorn the President's Room, where Chief Executives once came to sign bills in closing hours of Congressional sessions. Lincoln and others used the mahogany table. The artist labored some five years on the room's panels and borders. Here Senator Carl Hayden, Congress' elder statesman, meets reporters.*

115

VICE PRESIDENT'S office adjoins the Senate Reception Room. Here Chester A. Arthur repeated the oath as President after Garfield's assassination, and Henry Wilson died after "a congestive chill" suffered while tubbing in one of the Senate baths. Vice President Hubert H. Humphrey chats with Mrs. Humphrey and Sergeant at Arms Robert G. Dunphy. The ornate chandelier formerly hung in the White House.

PANELED ROOM created by East Front's extension gives Senators a place for special functions or private chats. Chaplain Frederick B. Harris meets with Senators John C. Stennis and Frank Carlson by its fluted mantelpiece.

flowers, and fruits, interlaced with scroll-work. In painstaking detail, he drew medallion portraits of famous Americans, intermingled with battle scenes, landscapes, and panels representing American farming and industry.

Outside the room once used by the Committee on Patents, you see Brumidi's study of Benjamin Franklin as scientist and inventor. Along this "Patent Corridor," he also paid his respects to Robert Fulton and John Fitch of steamboat fame.

You find the lavish hand of Brumidi again in the Capitol's two gilt-and-plush show rooms, located behind the Senate Chamber at either end of the solons' private lobby.

In the President's Room, Brumidi frescoed his own art gallery on square inch after square inch of ceiling and walls. In addition to panels showing the members of Washington's first Cabinet, he painted curlicued designs framing symbolical figures, pensive Madonnas, and—for good measure —happy cherubs.

Though Presidents seldom visit this room now, many Chief Executives, beginning in

the 1860's, sat at its "Lincoln Table," signing 11th-hour bills into law.

Less ornate is the Senate Reception Room, where Senators meet friends and constituents. But how, you may ask, did two 20th-century portraits get into the frames made long before by Brumidi?

The story goes back to 1874. "Sooner or later," the artist predicted then, the "disfiguring" spaces that remained among his panels "must be completed."

The time came in 1957, when a Special Senate Committee, headed by future President John F. Kennedy, chose five outstanding Senators of the past to be honored by portraits painted in the medallions.

The selection was "nearly an impossible task," Senator Kennedy wrote at the time, with "possibilities for endless controversy." In the end the committee recommended five: the "Great Triumvirate," Clay, Webster, and Calhoun, and leaders of later progressive and conservative forces—Robert M. La Follette, Sr., and Robert A. Taft.

Behind closed doors lie a pair of hallowed rooms, set one above the other at the east side of the original Senate wing. Used in turn by Senate and Supreme Court, these chambers hold memories of events that rocked the Nation and molded its destiny. They are not open to the public now, but Congress will soon be asked to vote on legislation to restore them for exhibit as they looked from 1819 to 1859, when the Senate occupied the upper room, and the Supreme Court sat in the ground-floor chamber.

The Court's quarters, said a New York correspondent in 1824, seemed "hardly capacious enough for a ward justice.... It is a triangular, semi-circular, odd-shaped apartment, with three windows, and a pro-

fusion of arches.... Owing to the smallness ... the Judges are compelled to put on their robes in the presence of the spectators...."

But the cases heard by the Court were of national significance, and fashionable Washington, lacking diversions of more cosmopolitan centers, found a substitute for theater in the eloquence of lawyers.

Here Webster in 1819 argued an important constitutional issue involving his alma mater, Dartmouth, and ended with the moving words: "It is, Sir ... a small college and yet there are those who love it."

The same room 38 years later heard Chief Justice Roger B. Taney read his

opinion in the Dred Scott case, denying Negroes the right to citizenship, and fanning the fires of North-South controversy.

During those years, the now forlorn and silent Old Senate Chamber overhead was echoing to the debates that marked the Nation's territorial and economic expansion. It heard Thomas Corwin of Ohio make his courageous, futile stand in 1847 against popular sentiment for the Mexican War. And it saw Corwin's prophecy come true that acquisition of land from Mexico would lead to disastrous sectional strife.

Indeed, it was in this very room, less than 10 years later, that Congressional conflict over extension of slavery in the new western lands reached a climax in the brutal caning of Senator Charles Sumner of Massachusetts by South Carolina Representative Preston S. Brooks.

The Civil War was an ominous shadow in 1859 when the Senate moved in ceremonial procession to its present Chamber in the extended Senate wing.

The following year the Supreme Court took over the remodeled Old Senate Chamber. There it remained for three-quarters of a century, before moving to its own headquarters nearby. The last major decision handed down by the Court in the Capitol came in May, 1935. It voided the New Deal's National Industrial Recovery Act.

All byways in the Capitol lead eventually to the two legislative chambers where America's representatives speak and vote in open meeting before the world.

Visitors taking the officially guided 25-cent tour of the building are admitted in groups to the galleries within these halls. Individuals can obtain passes from Members of Congress for the asking.

The House Chamber—139 feet long and 93 feet wide—is one of the world's largest legislative rooms. Here Representatives sit in rows of unmarked chairs, as in a theater without reserved seats. By tradition, however, and for convenience, Republicans group themselves to the Speaker's left, Democrats to his right.

In the smaller Senate Chamber, each Member has his own desk, also arranged by custom with Republicans and Democrats respectively left and right of the Vice Pres-

LINCOLN AND HIS CABINET *sit gravely in Francis B. Carpenter's portrayal of the first reading of the Emancipation Proclamation. The artist spent six months in the White House on the canvas, presented to Congress in 1878. Seated (from left): Edwin M. Stanton, Lincoln, Gideon Welles, William H. Seward, Edward Bates. Standing: Salmon P. Chase, Caleb B. Smith, Montgomery Blair.*

CHERUB AND EAGLE grace bronze railings of Members' private staircases in Senate and House wings. The French sculptor Charles Baudin modeled them in 1859 from designs by Architect Walter. Their style is reminiscent of Brumidi. The latter toiled on Capitol decorations through the administrations of six Presidents. Assistants mixed colors, painted backgrounds, or drew in outlines from his sketches, but Brumidi himself did the final finishing.

ident. On each Senator's desk, this tradition-loving body keeps a crystal shaker of blotting sand as a memento from the quill-pen era. Under the desks gleam polished cuspidors. And on small marble ledges flanking the rostrum rest two tiny lacquered snuffboxes, recalling the hearty sneezes that yesteryear's legislators considered an inducement to clear-headed eloquence.

Visiting constituents, who may sometimes wonder at the casual atmosphere or lack of attendance in today's House or Senate Chambers, are reassured when they learn that most of the labors of Congress are performed in committees. As Woodrow Wilson wrote, "Congress in session is Congress on public exhibition, whilst Congress in its committee-rooms is Congress at work."

Important legislation, however, brings Senators and Representatives hurrying to record their yeas or nays. When the atomic test ban treaty came up for Senate ratification, all but one of the 100 Senators were in place. The missing Member was seriously ill in a hospital.

But there is still another side to the Capitol, behind the marble miles of show pieces and the public acts of Congress. You find this side in a working world of men and women whose job behind the scenes is to preserve and maintain the vast home of Congress and to keep its legislative mills forever grinding.

BRILLIANT TRACERY draws the attention of visitors in the "Brumidi Corridor" on the ground floor of the Senate wing. Here the artist painted walls and ceilings with birds, flowers, medallion portraits, and drawings of important inventions. Glazed Minton tile patterns the floor.

The Capitol at Work

"THE CAPITOL is a little city in itself," wrote a knowledgeable Washington newspaperman, Frank G. Carpenter, back in 1883.

It still is, only more so, as Congressional chores and needs expand to meet the increasing demands of modern legislation.

Off corridors of the Capitol complex, crowded with passing throngs, you find post offices, ticket and telegraph offices, disbursing offices, stationery shops, snack bars, cafeterias, and restaurants.

The Capitol maintains its own carpenter, electrical, and machine-repair shops, its own libraries, purchasing offices, warehouses, printing, mailing, and packaging rooms. It has its own barbershops, and there are beauty salons in the office buildings. A Capitol police corps, augmented by details from the District of Columbia police, guards the building and grounds. A medical officer and two other physicians staff first-aid rooms and offices for consultations and emergencies.

There is even a Prayer Room, established by a concurrent resolution of House and Senate in 1954. The small chamber is severely simple, and nondenominational. Anonymous donors presented the Bible, candelabra, flower vases, United States flag, and stained-glass window showing George Washington's kneeling figure.

Many Senators and Representatives have come to this quiet room of meditation and prayer since it was opened in 1955. And the number increases, attendants report, when crucial bills are up for decision.

"The late Senator Carter Glass once said that in 28 years he had never known a speech to change a vote," a Congressman recently told a group of friends. "But I know of several colleagues whose votes changed after visits to our Prayer Room."

Congress' working quarters are scattered from its debating halls to the farthest corners of its office buildings.

Immediately surrounding the formal Chambers are the legislators' private lobbies and cloakrooms, while beyond stretch mazes of administrative and clerical offices.

The word "lobbyist" came from such legislative anterooms, in which special pleaders sought to influence lawmakers. The term "lobbying" was current in the Capitol as early as 1832. During the heyday of railway expansion, the practice was so effective that Vermont's Senator Morrill once sarcastically proposed appointing a committee to consult with a railway president waiting in an outer lobby, to learn whether or not he wished any further legislation.

Rules for admitting outsiders to the floors of House and Senate have varied sharply through the years. During Senate debates on the Missouri Compromise in 1820, gallant Vice President Daniel D. Tompkins invited so many ladies into the Chamber that they filled all available seats and "got literally on the floor, to the no small inconvenience and displeasure of many gentlemen," a commentator reported.

When Congress holds a session today, only officially authorized persons may come onto the floors. All others are rigidly excluded—not only from where Congress sits, but from adjoining rooms as well.

At other times, visitors privileged to view the deserted House and Senate apartments

PRAYER ROOM *stays open at all times to legislators from both houses during sessions. President Washington in his Farewell Address labeled religion and morality "a necessary spring of popular government." His kneeling figure in the Prayer Room's stained-glass window has around it the 16th Psalm's "Preserve me, O God, for in Thee do I put my trust." Senator Claiborne Pell shows the room's massive Bible to his family.*

CHANDELIERED OFFICE *of the Senate Majority Leader contains a portrait of Henry Laurens, Revolutionary patriot, painted in 1781 during his imprisonment in the Tower of London. Noted John Singleton Copley was the artist.*

The Majority Leader holds a key post in Senate affairs. Chosen by his party's members, he guides legislation, speaks frequently in debate, helps shape policy. In this photograph Democratic Leader Mike Mansfield drafts a floor speech.

see them as stage settings from which the actors have departed.

Along the walls of the narrow Speaker's Lobby behind the House Chamber, you find portraits of 43 Speakers, from Frederick A. C. Muhlenberg to Sam Rayburn.

Muhlenberg of Pennsylvania presided over the infant House of Representatives in 1789, a month before President-elect George Washington was inaugurated. Like many early political leaders, Muhlenberg had served in the Continental Congress. He gave up a career as a Lutheran minister to take part in the affairs of the Nation.

Nathaniel Macon, Speaker in Jefferson's time, and fifth in the line of portraits hanging in the lobby, called the Speaker "the elect of the elect of all the people."

When you look at Henry Clay's thin, intense face here, you recall the young War Hawk who was chosen to preside on his first day in the House, and who served as Speaker through virtually all of his six terms as a Representative.

Strong men in the Speaker's chair have endowed the office with great prestige and immense power to influence legislation.

Studying the portraits of "Czar" Reed and "Uncle Joe" Cannon brings back the vanished eras of the 1890's and early 1900's. Then these two autocratic Speakers were admired and feared for their ruthless exercise of power through committee appointments and other parliamentary tactics.

The painting of bearded Speaker Cannon looks surprisingly mild for the man who clung fiercely to his dictatorship until a 1910 resolution, pushed through by a coalition of rebels, changed the House rules.

In Speaker Reed's portrait, painted in 1891 by artist John Sargent, you see a massive, egg-bald man with a drooping mustache. Said Reed when he was shown the painting, "all my enemies are revenged."

Portraits of Speakers Joseph W. Martin, Jr. and John W. McCormack have not yet been hung in the House lobby; likenesses go up only after the leaders have left Congress.

The last painting on view is that of the man who was Speaker longer than any other in history—Sam Rayburn of Texas.

When the able "Mr. Sam" earned the distinction of having presided more than twice as long as Clay, the previous record holder, the House held a special ceremony of congratulations and appreciation.

Dozens of Representatives spoke of Rayburn's parliamentary genius; of his integrity, impartiality, and kindness to new Members; of the bills vital to Americans that he had shepherded into law.

"I trust that those who follow us will know the history of our institutions and keep this Government free," he said in his response. "It is a tremendous honor for anyone, man or

ARCHED CEILING *and marble fireplace grace the Senate Minority Leader's office. As his party's chief in the Senate, the Minority Leader directs floor strategy, takes part in debate, and guards opposition interests. He and the Majority Leader occupy front row desks in the Chamber on their party's side of the center aisle.*

Constituents' letters pour into legislators' offices. Here Minority Leader Everett Dirksen dictates an answer. The portrait on the wall behind him is based on a famous photograph of Lincoln and his son Tad by Mathew Brady.

COMMITTEES SHAPE *most of Congress'*
work; no other legislative system gives
them such power. The Committee on
Foreign Relations includes (from left,
clockwise): Senators John J. Williams,
Carlson, Aiken, Hickenlooper, Fulbright
(Chairman), Sparkman, Mansfield, Morse,
Gore, Lausche, Symington, Clark, Pell,
Cooper, Case, and Mundt. In the
background are staff members
Bowman, Marcy, and Kuhl.

woman, to be elected one time to any office
within the gift of the people."

On the Senate side, opening off the main
lobby outside the formal Chamber, the
solons' Marble Room is in keeping with
the dignity of that august body. Variegated
Tennessee marble lines the walls; columns
of white Italian marble support a ceiling
paneled in identical stone.

At either end of a 64-foot expanse, gilt-
framed mirrors repeat in endless succession the room's rich red carpets and crystal
chandeliers. Magazines and newspapers on

mahogany tables heighten the clubroom flavor. Senators jealously guard the privacy of their Marble Room; so much so that they have officially designated it part of the Chamber itself. But this hall has seen its lighter moments.

In earlier times, when pages were younger and authorities more tolerant of pranks, the messenger boys used to meet here for "a council of the pages," a former Senate page recalled in memoirs published in 1886. Busts of two Indian chiefs adorned the room; on one "venerable Indian head" the group's

chief executive "used to sit when presiding."

Next door, the office of the Vice President contains a number of historic and even priceless objects. From one wall Rembrandt Peale's famed portrait of the first President looks down. The room's chandelier once hung in the White House. A gilt mirror above the fireplace supposedly belonged to John Adams. A smaller mirror, says a tradition passed along by old-time employees, was bought in Paris by Dolley Madison. Displayed here, too, is the marble bust of Grant's Vice President, Henry Wilson, who died in the room in 1875.

THOUGH the Capitol takes pride in its splendid rooms, lawmaking, after all, is its basic function. And today's legislative and related tasks have become so complex that it takes more than 7,500 men and women, working here and in the office buildings across the way, to help the 535 Members of Congress keep up with their jobs.

Each Member has his own office staff, including usually an administrative assistant and secretarial and clerical help. He has at his call the Legislative Reference Service of the Library of Congress, to look up for him information on any subject under the sun. And he can turn to the Office of the Legislative Counsel for a helping hand in legal fine points of wording a bill.

The committees he may serve on—Congress has 30-odd standing committees plus scores of subcommittees—employ batteries of technical people to advise him on bills dealing with anything from flood control to space flight. In addition, Senate and House have legislative and administrative staffs—headed by the Secretary of the Senate and Clerk of the House—that include document superintendents, financial clerks, librarians, and others. Their knowledge of Congressional functions and traditions is essential to carrying out the legislator's will.

Yet despite all such aids, only the Member can attend to many matters. He must see visiting constituents and perform various informational and other services in behalf of state and business interests back home. Dictating letters is another big item. According to one estimate, handling the mail accounts for about 80 percent of the work

load in the average Congressional office.

As one observer of the Nation's legislative process put it: "No king ever wielded a scepter more powerful than a nickel pencil in the hands of an American voter." And from the voters more than 2 million letters a month pour into the post offices of the Capitol and its related office buildings.

Topics covered by Congressional mail are as varied as the people they come from. Writers may ask help in obtaining Social Security benefits, a job with the Peace Corps —or advice on how to find a runaway husband. A would-be inventor once asked his Congressman to please send him a list of everything that had not yet been invented.

Members of Congress welcome opinions on pending bills or suggestions for needed legislation. But they are quick to spot the identical phrasing in letters and telegrams that reveals the organized efforts of pressure groups. Legislators are glad to inform youngsters on the workings of Government, but they are sometimes swamped by children's requests, in effect, for someone else to do their homework.

Letters may contain bouquets of praise. Or, more often, brickbats. Congressmen wryly point out that a favorite comment from disgruntled humorists suggests the erring legislator has a great future—in some other profession.

Occasionally the temptation is strong to talk back. One Representative contented himself with two words in replying to an irate constituent who had threatened to move to Canada. "Bon voyage," he wrote.

Another part of a Congressmen's job is the time-honored practice of sending out Government bulletins on progress in farming, industrial developments, baby care, and other subjects of interest to constituents.

As sessions of Congress run longer and longer, Members lean more and more on modern forms of communication to keep in touch with the people back home. One such device is the chatty weekly or monthly newsletter, containing facts and comments on the Washington scene.

For other links with the home front, Congress offers legislators the use, at cost, of recording facilities for radio and TV. In studios set aside on the Hill, Congressmen prepare regular or special programs. These may be interviews on current events, round-table discussions, or reports to constituents. The tapes and films go to local stations for broadcast to the public.

Faced with all these auxiliary activities, a Member finds his day crowded. "Fifty years ago," writes George B. Galloway, Senior Specialist of the Legislative Reference Service, legislators met in session "only nine months out of twenty-four. . . . The mail they received then referred mostly to free seed, rural routes, Spanish War pensions, and occasionally a legislative matter."

Today, Congressmen must consider the complex aspects of a mass of legislation constantly being suggested—in messages from the President, reports from Government agencies and departments, or petitions submitted by private groups or individuals. They must be prepared to defend their voting records before constituents who have access as never before to information provided by newspapers and other media.

You could write a book (people have) on how a proposal becomes law. The process takes as many as 28 stages. And House and Senate go about the business differently because of variations in size, nature, and traditions of the two Chambers. But, shorn of details, the basic steps are these:

A House Member drafts a bill—say, one providing a small land grant to a needy Indian tribe in the Southwest. He drops it into the House "hopper" at the Clerk's desk. Then the Parliamentarian refers it to the appropriate House committee—in this case, Interior and Insular Affairs.

The committee, or perhaps a subcommittee, considers the measure. It may call in consultants: Indian experts of the Department of the Interior, or advisers from the Bureau of the Budget, for example. It may hold public hearings at which witnesses for or against the bill can present their views.

On important and controversial measures, such hearings attract intensive news coverage. So do the investigative hearings Congressional committees also undertake. These need not stem from consideration of a bill; instead, they often result from a determination to look into a topic in pursuit of Congress's "watchdog" function. Since World War II, use of this powerful tool has expanded mightily.

COMMITTEE action may shape the Member's bill for return to the Clerk and placing on a House calendar. Or it may result in the bill's death—most measures introduced never complete the legislative process. Of 26,666 bills and resolutions proposed in 1965 and 1966, only 1,283 became law. Woodrow Wilson wrote that a bill killed in committee has crossed "a parliamentary bridge of sighs.... The means and time of its death are unknown, but its friends never see it again."

A bill reported out and put on a House calendar usually comes up for debate. Discussion may be routine; committee work and planning by party leaders often govern the bill's fate on the floor. Or debate may be lively—with oratory ranging from dull to inspired, and orators from little noted to long remembered.

Felix Walker, a legislator of the 1820's, became known as "old oil-jug" because of profuse speeches made—as he said—for Buncombe County in his North Carolina district. This put such words as "bunkum" and "debunking" in our language.

House rules now limit the time a Representative may speak in debate. Senators are

privileged to—and sometimes do—talk around the clock. In both houses, everything said is recorded by official reporters. They work at the bottom dais of the rostrum, or move to where speakers stand so they may catch each phrase.

In the old days of steel penpoints, some stenographers worked with tiny ink bottles strapped to their fingers. Today they use pen and notebook—though in special situations a shorthand machine may appear. Reporters record in relays, five or ten minutes at a stretch. The short intervals are

necessary to maintain the remarkable speed with which the Members' statements are transcribed, submitted to them for "revision and extension," and sent nightly to the Government Printing Office for inclusion in the next morning's edition of the *Congressional Record*.

This unique publication, which succeeded a report of debates in 1873, has a daily circulation of 49,000 copies. Each issue averages 160 pages of small print. It is bound as a "paperback" each two weeks, and in hard covers yearly. The *Record* for

COMMITTEE ASSIGNMENTS *give Members varied roles in legislative affairs. The House Rules Committee controls flow of bills to the floor. Its 15 members (from left, seated) are Reps. H. Allen Smith, John B. Anderson, Martin, Quillen, Latta, William R. Anderson, Matsunaga, Pepper, Young, Sisk, O'Neill, Bolling, Delaney, Madden, and Colmer (Chairman). Counsels Battle, Forrest, and Hynes stand. The gilded mirror dates from the 1850's.*

131

CONGRESSIONAL PAGES *run errands for legislators, go to school from 6:30 to 10:30 a.m. on the Hill. Here House Doorkeeper William M. Miller, whose duties include charge of House pages, oversees a payroll signing.*

CAPITOL POLICE *line up for a roll call. Duties of the 361-man force—besides guarding the building and maintaining order— include directing tourists, even running a lost-and-found service. Appointed by Congressmen, the men get special police training. Many are students working for degrees, particularly in law.*

FLOOR-TO-CEILING *files crowd the House Document Room near Statuary Hall. Here measures are card-indexed and kept for use by the current Congress— later to be sent for storage to the National Archives, Library of Congress, or basement and attic nooks about the Capitol. As many as 20,000 bills may be introduced in a single session of Congress; of them, perhaps 1,500 become law.*

POST OFFICE *and other services give the Capitol the facilities of a small city.*

CONGRESSIONAL RECORD *provides a journal of Congress' doings—some 160 pages a day.*

BANKING SERVICES *are offered at the House Sergeant at Arms' office, visited here by Rep. L. Mendel Rivers (right).*

TV STUDIOS *—with photo backdrop—and radio rooms in the Capitol get heavy use. Here Senators Clark and Scott interview a guest.*

the two sessions of the Eighty-ninth Congress filled 70,000 pages—not only with speeches made on the floors, but with material of all kinds that Members are permitted to insert in the publication's *Appendix*.

Congressmen have long joked about these *Record* supplements that may include anything from poetry and recipes to pages of statistics. Speaker Champ Clark disapproved of printing "articles and speeches not delivered in the house," but concluded "it was preferable to let them be printed rather than be compelled to listen to them."

The *Record* is the official journal of what takes place in daily floor sessions (accounts of committee proceedings appear as separate publications). It duly notes progress as a bill goes through reading, debate, and perhaps amendment in the House. The bill then comes up for vote. Passage sends it to the Senate—for another routine of committee study, floor debate, and voting.

Differences in a bill as passed by House and Senate may be accepted by the originating body, or worked out in a conference committee of Members of the two Chambers. Either house, of course, may originate a bill—with the exception, stated in the Constitution, that all revenue bills shall begin in the House.

Once final approval is voted in Senate and House, the bill goes to the President, whose signature makes it law. Should he return it to Congress with a veto, it can still be enacted—and printed for inclusion in statute books across the land—by a two-thirds vote of both houses.

FROM THE GALLERIES, visitors see the surface pageantry of this complicated process. In their respective Chambers the Speaker of the House and the President of the Senate call the sessions to order, usually at 12 noon. Chaplains offer a prayer before the day's work begins. Clerks read bills and record votes. Parliamentarians advise on rules and precedents. Members who hold the important posts of Majority and Minority Leaders and Whips direct strategy in carrying out the legislative aims of the political parties they represent.

Just learning the established procedures by which Congress conducts its business

SUBWAYS *whisk passengers from Senate and new House offices to the Capitol.*

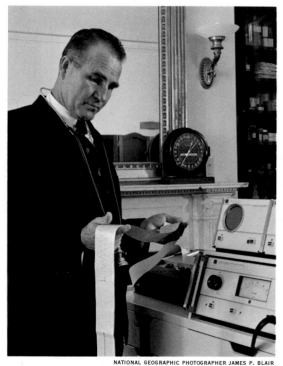

CAPITOL PHYSICIAN *Rufus J. Pearson checks an electrocardiogram; his office looks after the legislators' health.*

135

is an undertaking in itself. Freshman Senators and Representatives, old hands say, need at least a full session merely to grasp the intricate rules and customs they must follow. As Speaker Clark put it: "A new Congressman must begin at the foot of the class and spell up."

Recently, however, an informal seminar, organized by seasoned House Members on a nonpartisan basis, has offered newly elected Representatives a quicker insight into Congressional workings. Subjects include parliamentary practices, legislative ethics, and ways for beginners to take effective part in proceedings.

When Congress is in session, no offices are busier behind the scenes than each Chamber's Document Room.

Through these rooms flow endless streams of bills. They are indexed, filed, and kept up to date as action on them is taken. Subjects may range from an appropriation request to proposals for a national week in honor of high-school journalism or country music.

Distributing current bills from the Document Rooms is a daily task of the Capitol's youngest employees, the

SENATE RESTAURANT *serves legislators and their guests. Famed bean soup is a daily menu item, also flaky apple pie. Capitol cafeterias are open to the public.*

BRUMIDI PAINTING *in the House Restaurant shows Washington at Yorktown. On the briefcase strap at the lower right the artist lettered his grateful "Citizen of the U.S." signature note.*

Congressional pages. These boy messengers —50 for the House, 26 for the Senate— prepare the Chambers before each day's session. They see that legislators' desks are supplied with needed materials—and that the Senate snuffboxes are properly filled.

When sessions open, the pages sit on the steps of the Senate rostrum and on benches in the House—ready to run errands should Senators snap their fingers, or lights begin flashing on House signal boards.

Boy runners have been used in the House since Congress moved to Washington. The first recorded Senate page, a nine-year-old protégé of Clay and Webster, was appointed in 1829. Today's pages are older (14 to 18), but still are chosen by Members. The job carries considerable prestige and pays $4,905 a year. But the post is no sine-cure. Before reporting for daily work, pages must attend a Congress-supported high school whose classes begin at 6:30 a.m.

Like the pages, members of the Capitol's 361-man police force are appointed by Members. They are said to be the world's best educated policemen. Most are graduate students working toward advanced degrees.

The Capitol corps, augmented by a few men detailed from the District of Columbia force, has the usual police duties—plus some distinctly unusual. Officers often escort visiting celebrities—reigning monarchs or beauty queens—on tours of the building. And picking up after 40,000 visitors on a holiday can bring problems to the lost-and-found department at police headquarters.

Capitol police may have to deal with occasional disturbances by angry—or mentally ill—onlookers. But the only truly violent outbreak among spectators in Capitol his-

tory came in 1954, when four Puerto Rican nationalists suddenly began firing from a public gallery into the House Chamber below. Five Members were wounded.

The Puerto Rican attack made a dramatic eyewitness story for press representatives who happened to be on hand. But there is always news at this center of politics and government. So much so that more than 1,700 accredited correspondents and photographers are now provided with special galleries and offices from which to cover events. Opportunities to see and report on Congress at work have grown steadily through the years. In early decades, press coverage was not only limited in extent but

STEPS AND TERRACES *of the Capitol's West Front break the easy slope of Jenkins Hill. Government offices edge the grounds: the porticoed Supreme Court Building, the cupola-capped Library of Congress with its huge Annex and the privately endowed Folger Shakespeare Library, and three House office buildings named (left to right) for former Speakers Cannon, Longworth, and Rayburn. The same scene photographed in 1930 points up changes made over the decades.*

often frankly slanted to serve political interests. At times, conflicts between suspicious Congressmen and frustrated editors led to mutual recriminations. Congress was interfering with the rights of a free press, said the elder James Gordon Bennett of the New York *Herald* in 1841. Correspondents, said a Senator around that time, were "miserable slanderers," given to "vile . . . misrepresentation of the proceedings here."

To the newsman today, few places in the world offer a better vantage point from which to record history in the making.

Here, too, the past has a way of cropping up, as in the discoveries, not long ago, of priceless documents. One, found in a storeroom over the Old House Chamber, turned out to be an engrossed copy of the resolution declaring war against Great Britain in 1812. Others were yellowed papers, tied with faded red tape, and tucked in an "empty" cabinet of a Senate attic. Dealing with earliest affairs of the Republic, some were signed "G. Washington," "John Adams," and "yr.mo.ob.serv. Th: Jefferson."

It is such links between past and future that give the Capitol its greatest fascination for Americans.

"What is left for man to do?" asked Henry Watterson, Member of Congress and prize-winning journalist, in 1919. "With wireless telegraphy, the airplane and the automobile annihilating time and space, what else?"

Some of the answers to that question will be heard in this building—where "We, the People" speak.

MELVILLE BELL GROSVENOR © N.G.S.

LIGHTS AGLOW *in a rosy twilight, the Capitol looms over Washington buildings. This view was made from the dome of the Library of Congress*

Index

References to illustrations and accompanying captions appear in **boldface**.

Congress OF THE United

begun and held at the City of New-York, or
Wednesday the fourth of March, one thousand and seven hundre

THE Conventions of a number of the States, having at the time of their adoptic
or abuse of its powers, that further declaratory and restrictive clauses should be added: And as extending the ground of public confidence

RESOLVED by the Senate and House of Representatives of the Unite
concurring, that the following Articles be proposed to the Legislatures of the several States, as amendments to the Constitution of the Unite
said Legislatures, to be valid to all intents and purposes, as part of the said Constitution; viz.t

ARTICLES in addition to, and Amendment of the Constitution of the Un
of the several States, pursuant to the fifth Article of the original Constitution.

Article the first.... After the first enumeration required by the first Article of the Constitution, there shall be one Representative for every th
which, the proportion shall be so regulated by Congress, that there shall be not less than one hundred Represen
until the number of Representatives shall amount to two hundred, after which the proportion shall be so regulated
nor more than one Representative for every fifty thousand persons.

Article the second... No law, varying the compensation for the services of the Senators and Representatives, shall take effect, until an electi

Article the third...... Congress shall make no law respecting an establishment of religion, or prohibiting the free exercise thereof; or abridging t
assemble, and to petition the Government for a redress of grievances.

Article the fourth. A well regulated Militia, being necessary to the security of a free State, the right of the people to keep and bear

Article the fifth...... No Soldier shall, in time of peace be quartered in any house, without the consent of the Owner, nor in time of war, b

Article the sixth...... The right of the people to be secure in their persons, houses, papers, and effects, against unreasonable searches and
probable cause, supported by Oath or affirmation, and particularly describing the place to be searched, and the pe

Article the seventh. No person shall be held to answer for a capital, or otherwise infamous crime, unless on a presentment or indictment of a
Militia, when in actual service in time of War or public danger; nor shall any person be subject for the same offence
criminal case to be a witness against himself, nor be deprived of life, liberty, or property, without due process of lau

Article the eighth. In all criminal prosecutions, the accused shall enjoy the right to a speedy and public trial, by an impartial jury of
district shall have been previously ascertained by law, and to be informed of the nature and cause of the accusation;
for obtaining witnesses in his favor, and to have the assistance of Counsel for his defence.

Article the ninth. In suits at common law, where the value in controversy shall exceed twenty dollars, the right of trial by jury shall b
any Court of the United States, than according to the rules of the common law.

Article the tenth. Excessive bail shall not be required, nor excessive fines imposed, nor cruel and unusual punishments inflicted.

Article the eleventh. The enumeration in the Constitution, of certain rights, shall not be construed to deny or disparage others retained

Article the twelfth. The powers not delegated to the United States by the Constitution, nor prohibited by it to the States, are reserved

ATTEST,

Frederick Augustus Muhlenberg Speaker of the Hou

John Adams Vice-President of

John Beckley Clerk of the House of Representatives.
Sam. A. Otis Secretary of the Senate.